ARTHUR BEVIN

Upholstery

ARC BOOKS, Inc.

PUBLISHED BY ARC BOOKS, Inc.
480 Lexington Avenue, New York 17, N. Y.

Library of Congress Catalog Card No.: 62-17580

Printed in The United States of America

Contents

Acknowledgements

The photographs illustrating the completed chairs or suites in the plates section of this book were supplied by the respective manufacturers to whom grateful acknowledgement is hereby given.

CHAPTER ONE

Brief history

It is widely thought that the craft of upholstery evolved from that of the tent-maker. And it does seem a likely development. Although tent-making is now quite a separate and a very prosperous trade, it is not so many years ago that many branches of that trade were carried out by the upholsterer.

The Upholsterers' Company was granted a charter in the year A.D. 1626 and is one of the oldest of the City of London Guilds and Liveries Companies. Its coat of arms being a shield with three tents. It was first emblazoned in A.D. 1465.

One of the first developments from tent-making was 'wall hangings' and draperies at windows and around beds. This is a branch of the trade that has almost died out. At least the wall hangings and bed draperies. The window drapery has since grown enormously, incorporating jobs like blind fixing, loose-cover making and bed-cover making.

The first signs of comfort for chairs came with the making of cushions, but it was not until the reign of Queen Elizabeth I that the stuffing of furniture began to evolve. From then on the craft of upholstery increased and was in great demand, reaching its zenith probably in the late Victorian era and early Edwardian days.

By this time the standard of workmanship and versatility in England was really magnificent. It may well have surpassed the art of the French and Italian craftsmen who were considered supreme.

At this point it may be as well to point out and consider the numerous jobs that came under the proud title of 'journeyman upholsterer'.

Basically of course he was a 'stuffer', which really means an upholsterer as the layman knows it. In other words, he built up from a frame a piece of furniture padded with stuffing. He also undertook to measure, cut and fix curtains, blinds, draperies, loose covers and pelmets and swags. This included things like mantelpiece drapes and bed draperies which were very popular in those days. Indeed all types of draperies for furniture became most elaborate, as did the window dressings. Deep swags and tails for the window headings suited the tall windows of the wealthy client's house. These were usually heavily trimmed and sometimes surmounted by elaborate wooden cornices.

Floor coverings came under the upholsterer's jurisdiction. These included carpets, linoleum and art felts. And on a more macabre note, he lined coffins. Until the turn of the century hanging wallpapers was yet one more task in the furnishing trade that was carried out by this craftsman.

This may sound a pretty comprehensive list in these days of mass production and prefabrication and probably strikes one as being in the dim past. But I can still recall doing all these jobs, with the exception of wallpaper hanging, during my years of apprenticeship. My grandmother used to tell me that her father, who was an upholsterer, went to work in his top hat and spats which was a symbol of the prestige in which this craftsman was held.

The all-round upholsterer still exists today I'm glad to say, and is found usually in the good-class furniture retail stores of the provincial towns. The trade in London and the very big cities is split up into three sections, because of the volume of work carried out. The sections consist of Upholstery, Soft Furnishings and Carpet Planning. The first deals with furniture of the stuff-over type; the soft-furnishing fitter deals with loose-cover and curtain making, and the carpet planner measures and plans all types of floor coverings.

The amount of work in all these branches is so great that craftsmen in these jobs are very hard to get. The all-round man has to choose which branch to work at if he decides to make his living in one of the big cities. Conditions of working have improved tremendously, as they have for most trades. During the nineteen-thirties the 'stuffer', or 'ragtacker' as he is called, probably experienced the worst conditions. These were prevalent wherever there was great unemployment. 'Sweat shops' sprang up all over the country to keep pace with the 'Installment Plan Era' which had just started. A lot of furniture made in these workshops and factories was of the cheapest and poorest quality and the craftsman had to prostitute his skill in order to keep a job. Some idea of payment may be got if I tell you that $4 to $4.50 was an average rate for a small three-piece suite in leathercloth. This was for the finished job from frame to cover.

A lot of tedious jobs have been eliminated by the manufacture of spring units, ready shaped padding and rubberized hair that can be cut off a roll to a required length. There are also machines used in the trade, but for a first-class job it still remains a craft, where patience and skill of hand and eye play the most important part. Pride of craftsmanship is a great incentive to a beginner and the would-be apprentice should not think there aren't workshops that still carry on the traditions and skills. There certainly are! These skills are also taught in nearly every town or city that boasts a technical college, and apprentices can usually attend under the day-release schemes and also in the evenings.

In the following chapters we shall be dealing only with upholstery—the basic fundamental methods of turning out the quality piece of upholstered furniture. There is perhaps a sense of creation in upholstery that is quite different from woodwork or metalwork and as one reaches the final stages there is a great satisfaction. Particularly if the foundation is sound. The instructions in this book will, I hope, encourage the reader to achieve making that favourite piece of furniture.

CHAPTER TWO

Tools and workshop requirements

COMPARED with other trades like cabinet-making, plumbing, etc., the upholstery trade requires few tools.

Hammers

Perhaps the most important one is the upholsterer's hammer. Upholstery hammers are specially made for this specific craft. There are three types, the favourite one

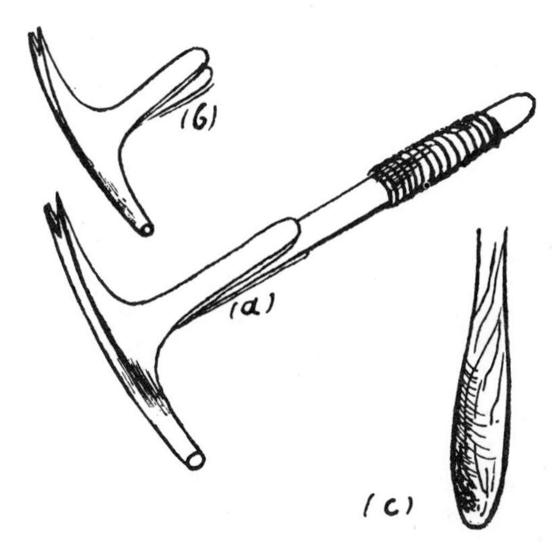

Fig. 1.
(*a*) Ringed shaft upholsterers hammer. (*b*) Head of cabriole. (Note small driving area). (*c*) Pear shaped shaft.

being that with the round ringed shaft. This is the better designed and balanced hammer and has a hardened steel tipped driving face. Another type has a pear-shaped handle and a more square-cut steel head. Both these are known as tack hammers. The remaining pattern is called a 'cabriole' hammer, the main difference being a much smaller driving surface—about a quarter of an inch in diameter, whereas the average tack hammer is about five-eighths of an inch.

The 'cabriole' is used mainly for 'show-wood' furniture where great care is needed when tacking, not to bruise or damage the surrounding woodwork. Hence the reason for the small head of the hammer. It is also used for 'gimping', the fixing of a finished braid or gimp by the use of gimp pins.

Cutting tools

These consist of scissors and knives, the former should be about nine or ten inches in length and of good quality. A first-class pair of scissors will last an upholsterer all his working life. Here again we have a choice of design. One type has a square end finish to one of its blades and the other type has a pointed end to both blades. The last-mentioned are particularly useful when cutting loose covers and usually are a little dearer to buy. A knife is an essential tool for 'trimming off' after the cover has been tacked on—particularly for hide and leathercloths. What kind of a knife doesn't matter, as long as it has a good sharp edge—any straight bladed knife made of good steel. Sharpen when necessary on an emery paper or whetstone.

Web strainers

The thing that puzzles nearly every amateur upholsterer is how to stretch the webbing tight. This is done by a web strainer or stretcher. There are one or two different types of these, as will be seen in the sketches.

All are made of hardwood, the simplest being a piece of wood with a groove at one end which fits over the edge of

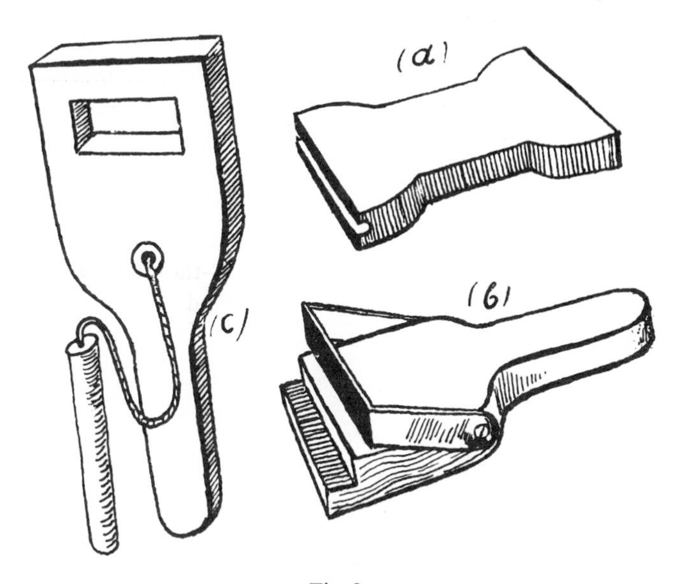

Fig. 2.
(*a*) Simple web strainer. (*b*) Lever type strainer. (*c*) Slot and rod type strainer.

the frame being webbed. The webbing is brought over the top and under the grooved end which is placed against the frame. With a firm handgrip it is levered downwards until the required tautness is reached. Another version, mostly used in America, is the one that has four or five spikes in the levering end. This does away with having to pass the webbing under the grooved end, but it can damage and weaken the webbing. The type of strainer that has the slot in the main body of the wood and a piece of dowelling or rod attached is one of the most popular. With the handle upright the webbing is passed double through the slot to form a loop. Through this loop is placed the dowelling or rod to hold it and the strain is applied in the same way. The last version is known as the lever-type strainer. This is a quick and easy method of web stretching. The webbing is passed over the lever and allowed to hang, the leverage is then taken up in the same way with the rebated end against the frame side and a downward pressure. Another form of stretcher is the web

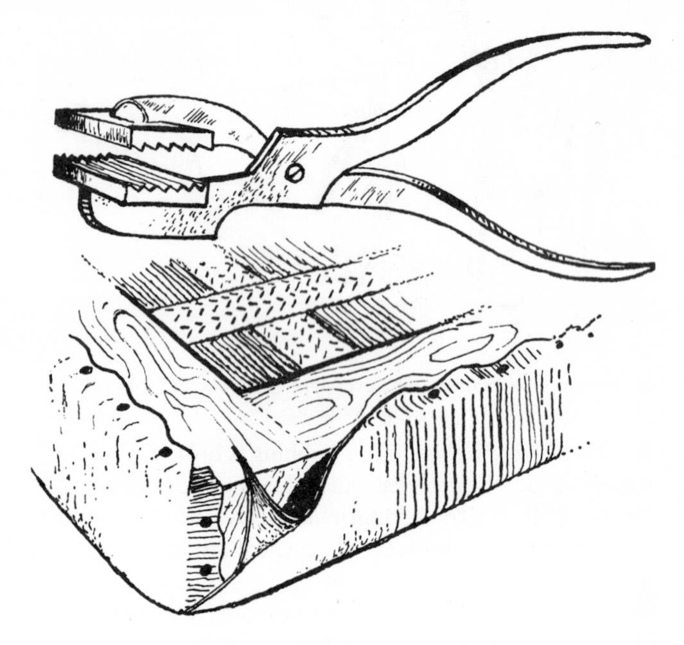

Fig. 3.
Finishing of corners. Web and hide stretcher.

or hide pincers. This tool, made like pincers, has wide serrated jaws and is useful for straining short ends of webbing or hides.

Ripping-out tools

These consist of an upholsterer's ripping chisel and a wooden mallet and are used to prepare the frame for a repair. The chisel end is placed against the tack and given

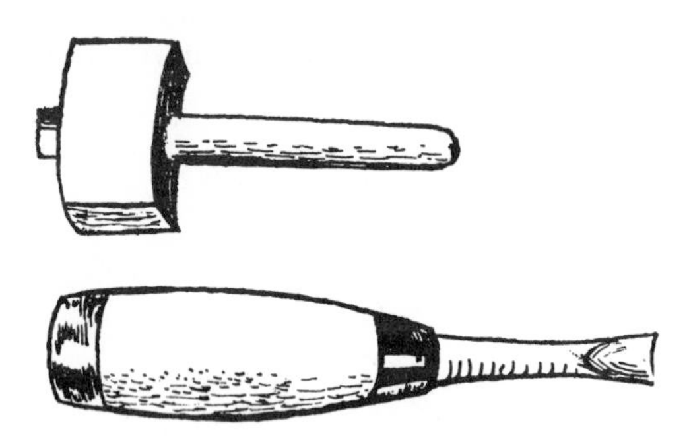

Fig. 4. Ring chisel and mallet.

one or two blows to remove same; always with the grain of the wood, otherwise you may crack or chip the woodwork. A 'wood rasp' is for rounding off corners of the frame where an 'edge' has to be tacked. Screwdrivers, pincers, and a bradawl complete the general tool layout.

Upholsterers' needles and stitching tools

These are essential requirements. They consist of mattress or stitching needles and are from 8 to 16 in. in length. They have double-pointed ends with an eye about an inch from one end and are round in section. An exception is the one that is shaped triangularly for about a third of its length. This is called a bayonet point. It is most useful for stitching built-up stuffed edges as the bayonet point is stout enough to use as a regulator—a 'regulator' being the tool used for trimming or regulating the stuffing to the required place beneath its hessian covering. It is an extra-thick needle-like tool with a point at one end and the other ends played out flat to help leverage against the side of the palm when using it. Another tool for adjusting stuffing is the stuffing iron. This is a metal tool with a fork-like end and mainly used in America.

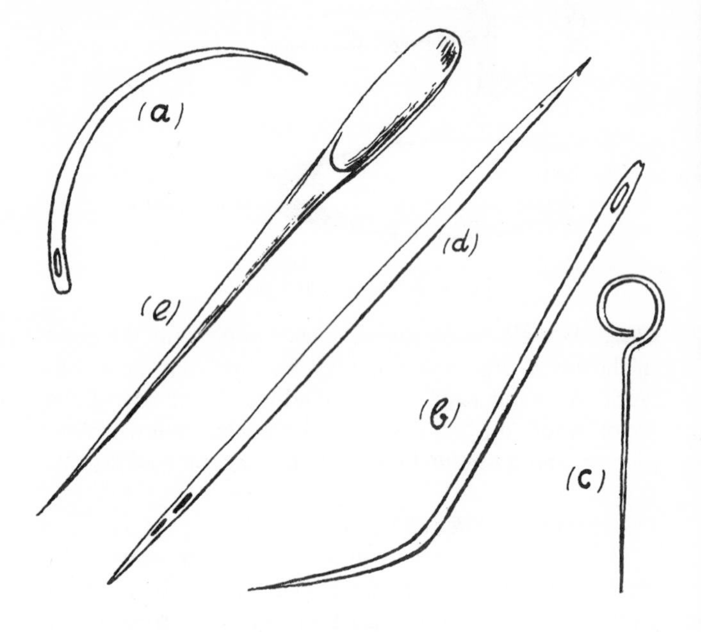

Fig. 5.
(*a*) Half-circular needle. (*b*) Spring needle or packing needle. (*c*) Skewer. (*d*) Stitching needle (8 in. to 14 in.). (*e*) Regulator.

A 'packing' or 'spring' needle and a half-circular needle will complete the stitching tools, a further addition being three or four dozen steel skewers. These are used to hold hessian or covers in position until they are stitched.

Machinery required for the workshop includes a heavy-duty sewing machine and a carding machine. The latter is used for 'teasing' and cleaning various stuffings from repair jobs. A cushion-filling machine is needed if a large volume of this work is done. Factory machines usually include mattress-making machines and a loose-seat machine, a fairly recent innovation.

A linen tack bag with three or four sections is required to hold the different sizes of tacks, and an upholsterer's apron which has a capacious front pocket. This pocket is invaluable to the 'ragtacker'. Tacks are held in the mouth and it is quite a shock when one first sees a handful of tin tacks thrown into the mouth. They are brought to the lips by teeth and tongue and taken by the thumb and forefinger of the hammer hand, still holding the hammer. Experience has proved that this is the fastest and most suitable method. The advent of the hammer with the magnetic head prompted some to alter their technique by placing the hammer head to the lips and carrying the tack to the job direct. Whilst talking of tacks it is interesting to note that in most workshops they are cleaned before use. This is one of the first jobs the apprentice is required to do thoroughly. A canvas bag is made about 2 ft. long and 6 in. wide. The sewn-up end is tacked against the wall somewhere about waist height. The tacks are put into the bag and then, gripping the open end in his fist to keep them from falling out, the boy shakes the bag to and fro for approximately ten minutes, very much in the same way that the ostler cleans harness parts. A good cleaning will bring the tacks out bright and free from rust. Telling the apprentice to sharpen the points was one of those old gags that every workshop played on its beginners.

There is a combination that is essential for each man in the workshop. This is a pair of trestles and a bench. The trestles are of the usual variety but with a beading round the top. This is to prevent pieces of furniture with castors fixed from moving off. The bench is usually about 4 ft. square and is placed on the trestle tops for doing loose seats or cutting out, etc. The old-type Gladstone bag was a favourite for carrying the tools in, and a hair cushion tacked upon the wall near the bench took care of the needles and regulator. A tape measure is often found draped around this cushion ready to hand when needed.

CHAPTER THREE

Types and styles of frames

THE frames of upholstered furniture are, as the name implies, the skeleton upon which the stuffing or padding is built. These frames are made of metal and of timber, the great majority of them from timber.

I suppose the first frame-maker was the cabinet-maker or chair-maker for as already explained the first sign of more comfortable seating was the addition of a cushion to the completed chair or settee. As it developed to the stage of all-over stuffing a quite separate craft of frame-making began to emerge and indeed to day it is a trade that is fully occupied.

Modern metal frames can be made from tubular or pressed steel, the joints being welded or riveted. Wooden inserts are added wherever tacking is required. Although these frames are strong and durable they are also heavy, and if the riveting begins to work loose or there is any weakness in the welding then it does mean an expensive repair. The complete chair or settee has to be stripped down and re-upholstered after the frame repair has been effected. Far more adaptable are the timber frames which also allow greater scope for any alteration in the finished style either when first made or at a later stage when repairs are being carried out.

The timber frames are usually made from birch, beech or oak and also from other hardwoods. Nearly all frames are assembled by dowelling the joints, the main foundation rails using four dowels at each joint and where there are lesser strains and stresses, two or three dowels will suffice.

Factors such as the width or thickness of rails and what they have to carry guide the frame-maker to turn out a dependable job. Frames that show part of the wood as a decoration (called 'show-wood furniture') call for a

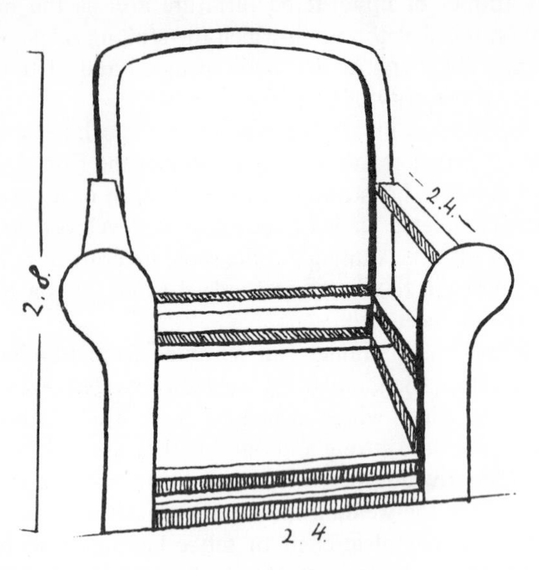

Fig. 6. Easy-chair frame.

degree of accuracy and skill comparable to a cabinet-maker's; particularly if it is a set of dining-chairs for instance.

A frame is more or less the shape of the finished upholstery, but a basic design can serve for several shapes by fixing extra shaped pieces of timber.

The ultimate aim of upholstery is to give more comfort, but of course if the frame-maker doesn't take into consideration things like the length of the seat in relation to the height of the arms and angle of the back, the finished piece may fall short of the comfort aimed at.

Frames that are to have spring units in place of webbing and coiled springs usually require fewer 'tacking rails'. These are the lighter rails above the stouter foundation timbers that are used for tacking canvases and covers, etc., to. The arm rail is also a little lower. Corner-strengthening blocks are advisable on all types of frames. These are triangular shapes glued and screwed at the angle of the main rails.

Settees with 'drop ends' are now obsolete and their place is taken by the modern bed-settee and studio couch. Although the bed-settee with the drop end was useful it was never popular with the upholsterer. It was most 'fiddling' to achieve a nice smooth job and except for the occasional visitor when they provided a bed, they had no other virtue. The best of the modern bed-settees are really first-class frame jobs, but of course do have various patented metal-made actions for converting from a settee to a bed. They also are first-class upholstery jobs.

The edges of frames that are to receive tacks should be rasped with a 'wood rasp' to round off the sharpness. The advantages of this will be seen as we proceed. A good frame-maker will be able to translate approximate dimensions of a desired style and proportion to your required finish.

CHAPTER FOUR

Springs and spring units

THE ordinary coil spring made of coppered steel is probably still the best and most efficient way of building a sound foundation. It is also the most adaptable unit in the comfort of an upholstered job. These are made in a long range from 3 in. in height to as high as 14 in. They are graded in gauges or thicknesses of the steel. The 3 to 8 in. are usually made in six gauges and the longer springs in four gauges and are the heavier types. The description given is 'three by fourteen' up to 'three by nine', the lower the gauge number, the heavier the wire, and consequently the harder the spring. For example, the 3 in. spring by fourteen gauge is much lighter than the 3 in. spring by nine gauge.

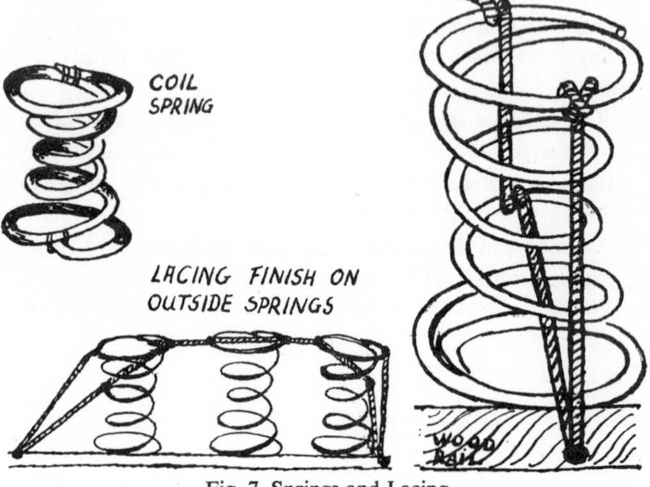

Fig. 7. Springs and Lacing.

The coil spring or double-cone spring has the centre, or waist, narrower than the ends. These ends of the wire are knotted to give a firm tidy finish. I mentioned the knotted finish as in America they also use open-ended springs quite a lot. Their system of cataloguing is usually from No. 00 to No. 6, representing springs from 4 in. to 14 in. high. They are classified as 'Furniture Springs', for seating, and 'Pillow Springs' for arms and backs; 'Cushion Springs' or 'Auto Springs' being used for car seating. The English system of gauging springs allows a greater degree of judging how hard or soft a seat or back should be, according to the type of furniture being made—the lower-gauge and stronger springs for the seating and the lighter springs for the arms and backs, etc.

In the United States they are sold by the pound, a bundle weighing about 50 lb. This then is the "common or garden" upholstery spring.

With the advent of mass production and prefabrication came the 'spring unit'. This is the complete foundation either for the seat, back or arms and is made in single, double or even triple layers for the seats at least. The spring unit is composed of single-cone springs riveted on to a base of thin steel laths. The tops of the springs are held in an upright position by a wire mesh with a heavier wire around the edges. Another method of joining up the springs is by metal clips. The second layer is usually comprised of ordinary coil springs directly over the single-cone springing and fastened in the same way. The metal laths or 'straps' are bent over at the front to fix on the face of the front rail.

The upholsterers' supply store has these units in a variety of sizes and components, depending on the quality of the finished job. An average price for a unit today might be $1.50 for a chair and $3 to $5 for a settee. Of course a great deal of layout time is saved by fixing the spring unit, and this coupled with their cheapness makes them popular with manufacturers. However

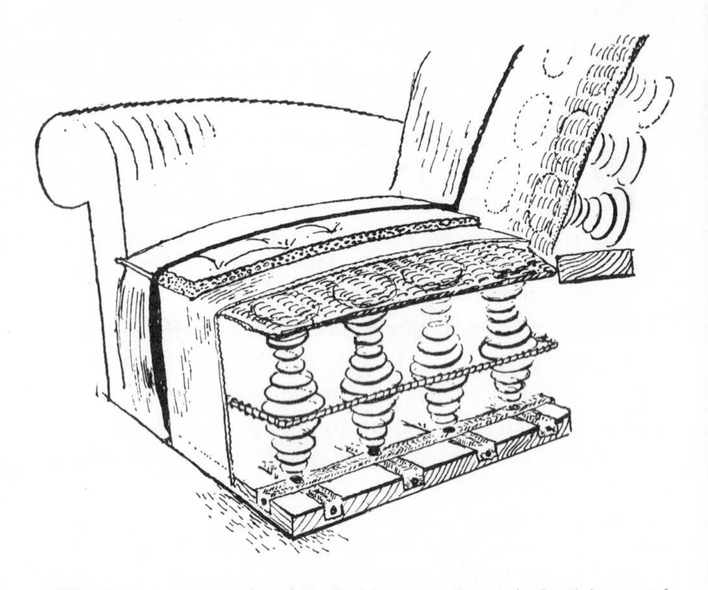

Fig. 8. A cut-away drawing showing a spring unit fixed by metal straps. Also showing the scrim stuffing.

they have their disadvantages. Perhaps the basic fundamental difference between these and a hand-sprung job is this: The coil spring is so laced together that when it takes the body weight the springs revert to an upright position. The unit springs do the opposite except at the point of impact of the weight. Thus if one sits in the centre the centre springs will depress straight down but the springs around them are pulled from the upright position because of the wire mesh or metal clips connecting them together. This tends to buckle them more quickly. Another fault seems to be the early tendency to squeak, and the bottom layer of springs hitting the metal webbing. This can be remedied however by stuffing a webbing or felt between the coils. Another type of spring unit of course is the cushion unit and the spring-interior mattress unit. These are usually pocketed in calico, the springs being 3 in. in diameter all the way down and clipped together. They are made up to any required size in multiples of 3 in. This is where the unit excels, as in these circumstances they are supplementary to a spring foundation and do not carry nearly the weight.

Other forms of springing widely used by all upholstery manufacturers are the cable spring and the tension webbing.

The former is made in the style of a cable and is anything from $\frac{3}{8}$ in. diameter to about $\frac{3}{4}$ in. and in gauges from fourteen to eighteen. It is obtainable in uncovered steel or plastic covering, and one well-known manufacturer has these springs cloth-covered together with a tape that covers the hooks after they are in position.

This form of springing is fixed to the side rails of the chair or settee which have been rebated or have had grooves put in to take whatever type of fixing is necessary. If there is a groove in the side rail then the hook of the cable spring is inserted and a nail driven from the top of the rail passing through the hook and groove. Metal plates can be used with holes already drilled; these are fixed on to the rebated edge of the rail. The tape method has eyelets already in the tape and this is attached to the rail by small nails around the eyelet. The hooks of the cable spring are then attached and the top tape covers the whole fixing, making it very tidy.

The tension webbing is about the same dimension as any other type and is made of good-quality rubber. The number used depends on the type of area to be sprung or the use it is going to be put to. This can be fixed in various

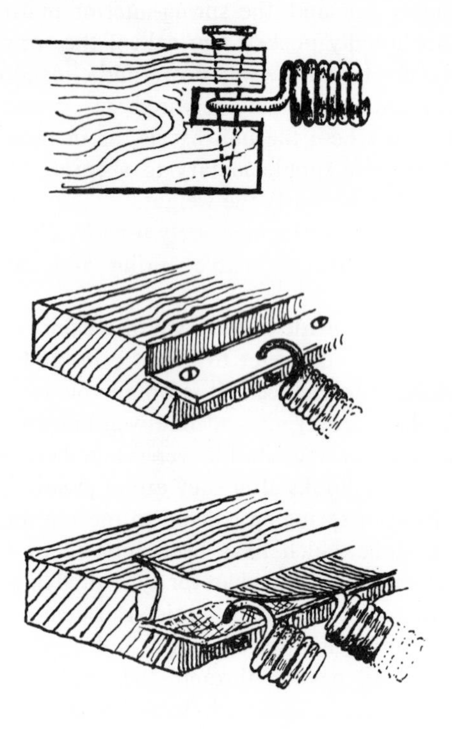

Fig. 9. Examples of cable springs.

ways such as tacking, screwing down under a plate or between an additional rail on the inside of the frame.

Perhaps the main difference between the orthodox springs and the ones just mentioned is that the cable and tension springs take the weight by expanding, whilst the coil-type springs compress when any weight is put upon them. However the cable and tension method is invariably used with a spring-interior or foam-rubber cushion and mostly on smaller-type furniture.

CHAPTER FIVE

Stuffing materials

Webbing

ALTHOUGH one can't classify webbing as a stuffing material I've included it in this chapter because it is upon the soundness and quality of webbing that any upholstered job depends. That is, of course, if it is not a spring-unit job.

Upholstery webbing is made in various qualities. The best-known and the highest grade is known in the trade as 'English Webbing' or 'Black and White Webbing'. It is made of pure flax in a herring-bone design of black and white. Lesser qualities have a percentage of jute, cotton or hemp and often a linen thread is woven to improve the selvedge strength. The widths run from 2 in., $2\frac{1}{8}$ in. and $2\frac{1}{4}$ in. and are bought in pieces. English webbing pieces are 18 yds. in length whilst the cheaper forms run to 36 yds. a piece. The lesser-grade webbing is plain brown in colour and striped. Made of jute throughout and imported from India comes a plain weave in widths from $1\frac{1}{2}$ in. to 3 in. This is possibly the cheapest of all webbings. Naturally the prices of these webbings are much below our webs.

In the United States jute webbing seems to be the usual foundation material and it is graded according to weave. The sizes are wider than ours and run from 3 to 4 in. A piece is 72 yds. in length.

For the webbing of any sprung seat the English web has no equal and when it is strained and tacked properly it will retain its strength and resilience for years. So it will be seen that careful consideration should be given to this part of the job if one is thinking of economies in any way. The jute variety can be quite adequate for inside arms and backs that are not to be sprung.

Burlap (Hessian)

The lightest or most-open weave of this material is known as 'scrim', and the heaviest or most closely woven is called 'tarpaulin' or 'spring canvas'. They are made in various weights and are all made from jute. The uses of burlap in the upholstery trade are many, and taking them more or less in their order we begin with the covering of the springs or webbing (if not sprung), for which the heavier grade is used, namely spring canvas. Then we come to the first stuffing, for which we use scrim. A medium-weight burlap is used for covering the bottoms of chairs, etc., and this can also be in black burlap. This covers the webbing and keeps the dust from falling on to carpets as well as putting a finishing touch to the job.

In England the popular width of hessians is 72 in., although many other widths are made. The U.S.A. seems to favour 40 in. as an average width. Also the name given to hessian is 'burlap' and referred to as eight to ten and a half, and twelve ounce weights.

Stuffings

These are numerous and varied and are obtained from animals, birds and fruit and even the sea. A sample list reads like this: hair, fibres, linsey wool, feathers, kapok and foam rubber. To the upholsterer, horse-hair, or hair as it is generally known, is the favourite and as yet there has not been another stuffing to equal it. It is the most resilient of stuffings, the best quality lasting for many years. It may instantly come to the mind that today foam rubber has surely displaced it. But this would not be right to assume. The finest-quality upholstered furniture still depends upon the great feel and skill of the craftsman. And it is the judgement very often, when stuffing, to know just how thick or dense to make 'first stuffings' and 'second stuffings' that gives the right firmness and shape. There are a number of qualities of hair, and also different-coloured hair. It is washed and sterilized and then spun into rope form. This twists the hair and gives to it the springiness that is its chief attribute. The longer the hair the more twist and resilience. A great proportion of this is dyed black. The rest is left in its natural colour and is known as 'grey hair'. Cheaper grades of hair are of the shorter length and are mixed with hog-hair and others not from horses.

The ideal stuffing is an all-hair stuffing but in many jobs hair is used for second stuffing only. Fibres of one sort or another are used for the first stuffings. The 'fibre' group is also greatly varied, the most widely used is probably black fibre. This comes from a process involving a North African dwarf palm tree. The leaves are split and dyed, but some left in their natural colour, green. An approximate price for this stuffing today is $18 a hundredweight bag.

Another vegetable fibre is the lining of the coconut husk. This has quite a curl in it which of course makes for more resilience. This is known as 'ginger fibre'. Both these

fibres make a very good first stuffing and stitched rolls or edges. The ginger fibre will make a firmer edge but tends to disintegrate more quickly with age. There is also a sisal fibre and a synthetic fibre but the latter does not seem to be manufactured these days. All the foregoing stuffings are now manufactured on stuffing pads, the stuffing being woven on to a hessian and obtainable by the roll or made to specially shaped templates. Another form of prefabricated pads uses latex rubber for binding the stuffings. Rubberized hair or fibre make for quick production. The less-expensive form of stuffing is black wool or flock and is manufactured from rags. This costs about $18 a hundredweight. The best is an excellent smooth and soft stuffing but of course without much resilience. The worst is really not worth buying and although the manufacturers have to meet a standard of cleanliness and quality to conform to the law, the lower-graded products leave much to be desired.
desired.

Rugging

Another form of stuffing is made from hessian jute scraps. Cotton flock is, as its name implies, made from cotton, and from cotton waste a useful material known as cotton linters. It is a felt made from linters in several qualities and widths and packed in bales of about twenty pounds weight. It is used as an alternative to wadding over the second stuffing and also as a lining around the spring units in cushions and mattresses. These then are the more robust stuffing materials.

At the beginning of this chapter I mentioned stuffing material coming from the sea. This was called, I believe. 'alva' and I can remember using it when an apprentice,

A repair job would often reveal the first stuffing was of alva. It was made from dried seaweed and made a very hard edge. Of course it is not used today but I can't help feeling that seaweed and many other things from the sea will in the future be processed for many things.

It looked at one time as though moulded rubber would supersede the fibres, but the manufacturing costs of this rubber seem to have safeguarded this. For as I mentioned previously the hand-teased hair stuffing is still supreme.

Feathers

Here again we have many qualities. Those plucked from the breasts of eider ducks are most expensive and are used mainly in quilts or eiderdowns. Duck and poultry feathers are washed and purified and are used for upholstery and they are nearly all imported.

Kapok

This is a popular stuffing or filling for smaller cushions, and is a vegetable from Java and the Dutch East Indies. This down is also used for life jackets.

Wadding

Made in sheet form of about 36 ft. long, wadding costs anything from 80¢ to $1.50 a piece. It is available also in 1 lb. packets. This is used to cover a second stuffing of hair or even over a calico covering. This gives a softness that is needed, particularly if a silk cover or something equally delicate is to be the final cover material. It also prevents the sharp ends of the hair stuffing from sticking through the covers.

Sundries

The sundries of almost every trade seem to be never-ending. The upholstery trade, being no exception, can catalogue numerous and well-assorted sundries. However, only the most important will be dealt with here. Two of the most important are tacks and twine.

Dealing with the **Twines** first, it might be as well to say now that there are usually at least three or four different qualities used in the making of a fully upholstered piece of furniture. Made from flax and hemp, it is often imported from Denmark and Ireland. The majority of hemp twine is Italian. Various thicknesses of twine are required to meet the needs of different jobs. We first use twine when sewing in the springs to the webbing. A medium thickness is wanted for this job and, as for all upholstery twines, one that doesn't twist too much. This is usually called 'spring twine'. A thicker quality is used when the springs are laced together and this is called 'lacing twine' or 'laid cord'. The twine or yarns are 'laid' together in a certain way which prevents stretch in the finished cord. This is most important as springs are laced to a set position and are under tension.

The twines for 'bridling' and 'stitching' are of a much finer variety. The stitching twine is pulled continually in the stitching process and is very strong. 'Piping' cords are used to insert in material to form a piped edging around such places as facings (the front uprights of the arm rail). These cords can be made from cotton or paper. Flax twines cost from $15 to $20 a dozen pounds, and hemp twine is a little cheaper. The first-grade hemp twine, however, can go to as much as $30 per dozen pounds weight. Laid cord is from $4.50 to $12.

Tacks. Fine or 'improved' tacks come in sizes from

$\frac{1}{4}$ in. to $\frac{5}{8}$ in. for upholstery work and are supplied in 28 lb. bags to the trade. They are also sold in 7 lb. packets. Gimp pins and round-headed nails with various finishes are also used for finishing off furniture. The former for gimp edging and the latter for leather bandings. The finishes for the nails are oxidized, brass, chromium and so on to coloured enamels. Studs can also be leather-covered. Upholstery buttons are used extensively. These have a metal backing with either a small ring or a cloth 'bos' and can be covered with any material required.

These then are the main sundries but of course from time to time extra sundries are called for.

CHAPTER SIX

Cover materials

IN choosing the type and quality of material to cover upholstered furniture, previous thought should be given to the value of the furniture and the usage to which it will be subjected, also to the general décor of the room it is to occupy. In the hey-day of upholstery the drawing-room was furnished with the finest linens and silks and the living-room with more robust materials such as tapestries and moquettes; or as they are called in America, mohairs.

Such rooms as libraries and studies had hide coverings for their chairs and settees and the 'club' chair was stamped by its size and hide covers. And indeed it still is a favourite in these days,

The drawing-room as such is almost extinct and its place taken by the combined dining-room and lounge. Smaller houses and shortage of staff have changed the layout of most family houses. The living-room is the centre of all family activity which in itself is probably a good thing.

With this in mind, the reader who has a family may well think that the only common-sense cover for his suite is real leather. However, owing to advanced methods of cleaning and maintaining materials, any hesitation or doubt is unwarranted.

Covers might be classified into three groups: hides, moroccos and leathercloth—pile materials—non-pile materials. The first group by their very nature are suitable only for certain kinds of jobs, such as already mentioned, club chairs, public house seating, transport furniture and so on. These can be covered in cowhide and sometimes pigskin or the manufactured leathercloth. Moroccos, however, are used more for finer pieces of furniture. Unfortunately they are out of fashion.

The area of a full cowhide skin is between 40 and 65 sq. ft. These are the largest skins and consequently give much less waste when cutting. They are very durable and modern methods of polishing and dyeing produce a beautifully soft hide. They are classified into two groups known as full-grained hides and buffed skins. The latter is the less costly of the two grades. It gets its name 'buffed' from the process of rubbing or buffing the hide with carborundum stone. This is carried out to obviate blemishes in the skin.

Cowhide can be purchased by the 'skin' or square foot. Morocco skins are the most durable and the finest of all skins used in the upholstery trade. They are the skins of goats and the best specimens come from the mountainous district of middle Europe. These animals carry very little fat content in their skins and this makes for very good wearing. From twenty-five years and upwards is a fair estimate of a morocco. They can be used with sheep skins which cover the outsides of a suite, i.e. the outside arms and outside back. Modern upholstery doesn't seem to find much use for them unfortunately.

The cutting of hides will be dealt with in a later chapter.

A product that has supplanted hide, or real leather, as the layman calls it, to a great extent is leathercloth. This is a fabric with a leather appearance and very often grained. It is bought off the roll like other materials in the soft-cover group. The best qualities of this material have a good finish and give first-class service. Hides and leathercloths require a very firm upholstery foundation.

Pile materials include velours and velvets and moquettes, of which there is a variety. Velours, the most robust type of velvet material, always produces an elegant-looking job. Its disadvantage is 'marking' with pile pressure. To minimize this, daily maintenance by a suction cleaner or soft brush is very helpful. Always finish this maintenance by brushing down the sweep of the pile. This can easily be detected by the palm of the hand and should always be sweeping towards the floor. The inside arms sweep into the seat.

Moquettes are manufactured in many designs and different finishes to the surface. The embossed moquette had great popularity in the thirties. The pile was cut away (or it appeared to be cut away) to leave a design in relief to the back of the cloth. Another popular covering and a very hard-wearing cloth was the uncut moquette.

Damasks and tapestries. What visions of luxury and good taste these names conjure up in the mind! These are the materials that stamp class on to many jobs. They are great favourites and of course they come in a long quality range. A good-quality damask with a self-colour design is probably the best choice to anyone aiming for good wearing qualities combined with elegance. Tapestries are not quite so durable but can be very attractive. A cheap quality is not to be recommended for furniture covering. Linens and cretonnes are used for certain pieces of furniture but they are mostly used in making loose'covers, or slip covers as they are called in Canada and America.

CHAPTER SEVEN

Measuring—cutting and preparing covers

MODERN upholstery factories carry out this part of the job on a very methodical scale. For each model of settee or chair, templates are made for every piece of cover, and several dozen pieces of cover are cut off with a machine. The number of cover pieces to a settee or chair is about ten. They are made up as follows: Seat—Inside Back—Outside Back—two Inside Arms and two Outside Arms—one or two Borders and two Facings.

In most workshops however the upholsterer cuts his own covers and as this is the most expensive material in the making of a suite, great care and thought should be given to this task before putting scissors to the cloth. The measurements should be written down against the parts concerned; e.g. Seat ....feet ....inches, I.B. ....feet ....inches, etc. Note the abbreviations which will continually crop up, amongst the cover parts. List vertically i.e. T.B.=Top Border. I.B.=Inside Back etc. Seat, I.B., O.B., I.A., O.A., Border, Facings. These symbols are chalked on the back of the pieces of cover for easy recognition. In the case of the I.A.s and the O.A.s it is as well to also mark them R and L (Right and Left). Some suites may well have a top border around the back and sometimes side facings on the back. Wings are yet other pieces that come with the winged armchair or settee.

The measuring should take place at the stage where either the first or second stuffing has been completed. If the second stuffing has a calico covering it is best to leave your measuring until this stage is reached. Depending on the type of weave the cover has, $\frac{3}{4}$ in. to 1 in. can be allowed for turns and seams, etc. This applies to the area that can be seen. However the seat, inside back and inside arms have the addition of 'flys' sewn on. This is the term given to pieces of canvas or old material which are sewn on to the edges of the cover that tuck down into the seat to reach the tacking rails. The upholsterer's American colleague refers to them as 'denim pullthroughs'.

These 'flys' or 'pullthroughs' serve two purposes, that of saving material and of giving better control of the material particularly when it is under strain. This applies more so when it is a patterned or an open-weave material. Any twist set up by pulling the material taut will finish where the fly meets the cover.

If the upholsterer has only one chair or settee he can by experience judge if he can get the material out of the yardage available, and usually he has estimated the job himself. However, if there are a number of pieces to be cut it is just as well to plan it out.

Take a large piece of paper and draw two parallel lines to a scale to represent a 50 in. wide material. The length of the lines should represent the length of material available, on the same scale. For example, if one works to the scale of 1 in. to 1 ft., then the lines will be just over 4 in. apart. And if the length of material is 12 ft. long, then the lines will be drawn 12 in. in length.

Once you have this rectangle set out you can refer to the sizes of each piece of cover and using the same scale draw them into the rectangle thus planning the most economical way of cutting. This way one also has the whole pattern before one which is useful when considering pattern or the brushing of pile. Another way is by cutting paper templates to the scale and this enables you to move them around within the rectangle plan. Remember 50 in. material includes the selvedges which can account for nearly 2 in. A more practical way is by cutting out to actual size using some old calico or hessian.

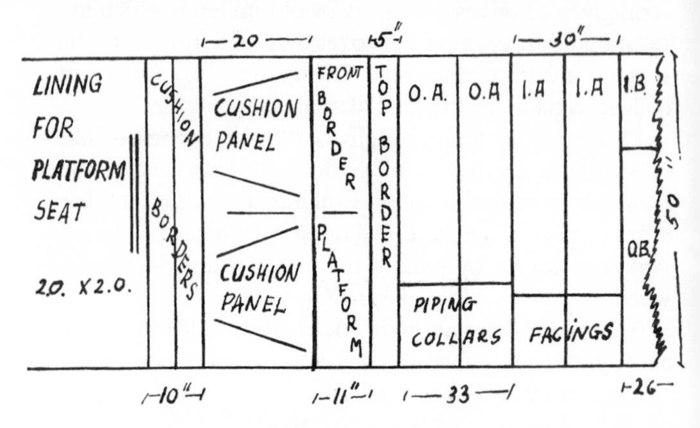

Fig. 10. Suggested way of planning covers.

These templates are then placed directly on to the cloth and planned and cut out that way.

It is as well to mention again at this stage the direction of pile or pattern. This invariably runs from the top of the piece of furniture towards the floor, i.e. down the inside back over the edge of the seat and down to floor level. Inside arms brush down into the seat, whilst all outside coverings and facings again sweep down to the floor. Furniture that has a separate long flat arm has the pattern or pile running from the back of the arm and over the front.

There are two parts of a settee or chair that should be paired exactly when covering with a patterned material.

These are the 'inside arms' and the 'facings'. Whether the cover has a frequent repeat pattern or a focal motif, care should be taken to assure the design appearing in the same place on both arms and facings. After deciding just how to place the pattern motif on these pieces, cut one and using this as a template place it on the appropriate part of the cover and cut the second one. But make sure that you cut these second pieces either 'face to face' or 'back to back' otherwise you will find that you have two right-handed or left-handed pieces. Another point to note when cutting the seat (or top panel of the cushion) and the inside back: if the material has a large motif see that it is centred on the back and seat pieces, and sometimes this needs to be noted even when cutting the front border. This gives a line of continuity of pattern from the top to the floor level. The same principle applies of course to the outside cover but can be ignored if it means a considerable saving of material. The average chair seat and inside back can be done with half a width of 50 in. material, so one can see that a material chosen with a large design in the centre can mean a lot of waste. Settee seats, inside backs and outside backs usually take one and a half to two widths to cover. A width is centred and side pieces are sewn on to obtain the required width. In the case of a two-pillow or three-pillow settee where the inside back is divided into separate sections, then of course any pattern must be centred on each section.

Another economy in cover material is the substitution of a lining material for the main part of a cushion seat, known as a 'platform seat'. This is a seat that is made to carry a cushion when finished. The cover material in this case only covers the edge of the seat extending for 5 in. or 6 in. under the cushions, whilst the remaining area under the cushions has the lining material. Of course this seat lining is a necessity for hide suites otherwise the cushions would slide. A word here about cutting the cushion covers. A template is cut of one panel and the remaining panel cut from it. Here again it is cut 'back to back' or 'face to face'.

Preparation

Furniture cords as a finish to the edges of a suite are no longer seen. Instead we have the 'piped finish'. This means usually that the arms and facings are sewn together in one with a 'piped' seam. Piping being a cord covered with the material. Similar treatment is given to the inside back and

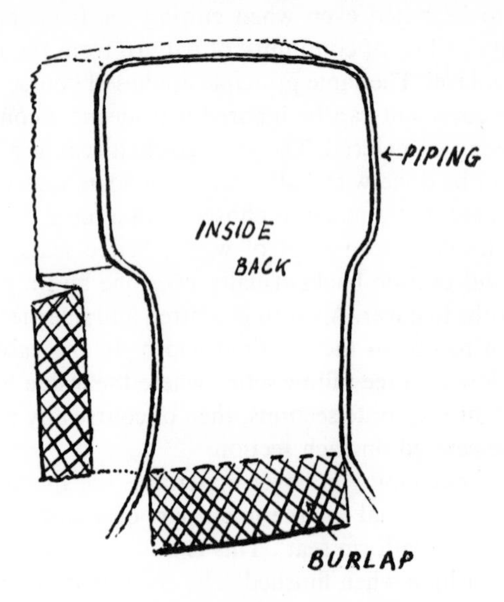

Fig. 11. Inside back cover prepared with piping and flys. Jacket style.

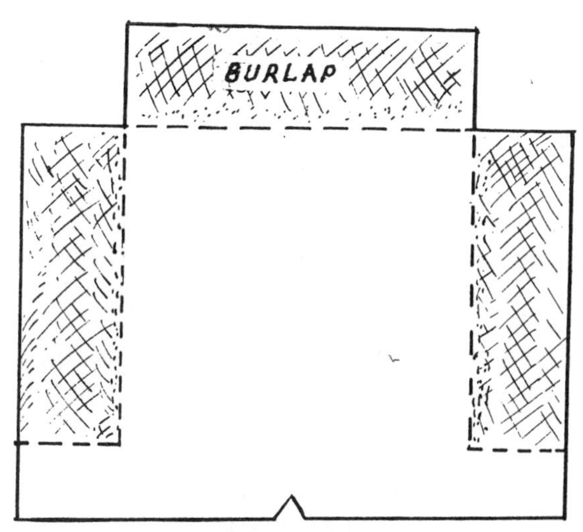

Fig. 11*A*. Seat cover with fly attached.

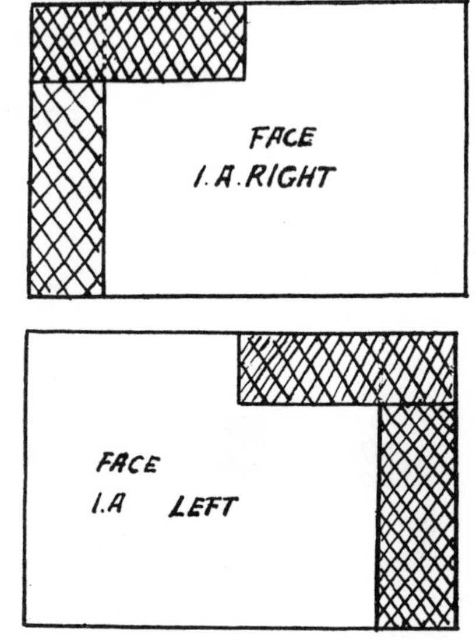

Fig. 11*B*. Covers for inside arms with flys.

the top border and the seat and front border. They are generally termed 'jackets'. These 'jackets' are pulled on and adjusted to their correct positions and tacked. This calls for strong wrists and sensitive hands. All hide or morocco jobs are done in this way, the facings usually being wood, with the hide tacked on before fixing. They are temporarily fixed in position and a hole bored through the facing and frame which is countersunk to take the head of a 'bolt'. The facing is removed and the bolt inserted in the hole, and then the hide, which has already been piped, tacked on to the facing. Before the outside arm is tacked the facing is replaced and the nut screwed to the bolt, thus securing it in position.

When cutting hides and moroccos the full-size template method is much better. Joins can be made on the outside covers by 'skiving' the leather. This is done by a sharp thin knife. A chamfered cut is made, about 4 in. in, on the

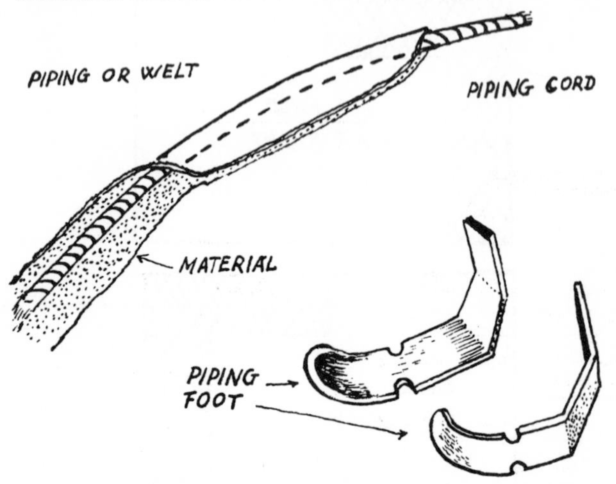

Fig. 12. Specimen of piping and a piping foot attachment.

back of both pieces of hide, ending the cut wafer thin. These two pieces are then glued together and layed upon a flat surface and weights placed on until firmly stuck. This is the method also for joining pieces of hide together for piping.

Piping with soft materials calls for strips an inch wide and cut on the bias. Cutting the material on the cross like this prevents any fullness when making up. A piping cord is layed inside, the material folded over the cord and machined along, using an attachment called a 'piping foot'. Occasionally when the cover is not 'jacketed' fullness around the 'scroll' (the circular shape in front of the arm) is dispersed by evenly placed pleats tacked against the facing. Or in the case of hide covering, tight folds are preferable. In either case no fullness should show on the top side of the scroll.

Machining

Half an inch is the standard allowance for joining and a double stitching row is advisable. When a 'deep-buttoned' job or a fluted method of covering is adopted, extra allowances must be made when measuring and cutting. Be generous, for a skimped cover looks conspicuous.

It will be seen that careful preparation is well worth while and can save a lot of time and prevent mistakes. When it comes to preparing the cover material it is a personal choice whether one prepares the whole number of pieces at one time or does each piece as one is ready for it. The former is advisable as the continuity of different physical actions makes for speed and perfection. However, as soon as staleness develops it is as well to leave off and switch to another task.

CHAPTER EIGHT

Basic principles of upholstery—priorities

THE object of upholstering a chair or a settee frame is to provide a comfortable piece of furniture to sit on or recline in. As it is more than likely that it will get regular everyday use it is therefore essential that it should have sound foundations. After the frame, the basic foundations are of two types; the 'webbing and spring' and sometimes just 'webbing and canvas' base. In common with most jobs of work, if we begin right it will serve as an excellent guide to all that will follow on. So the first part, the webbing, may well merit detailed explanation.

Webbing

There should be as many webs as possible, to carry the weight of the area with a spacing of approximately 2¼ in. between each webbing. This is equal to the width of a web, and a quick way to measure the distance is to place the web about to be tacked three fingers from the last. They are interlaced to give extra strength in unity in the same manner as an elementary weave. It is sometimes a practice, when webbing a large seat area, to web double. That is, to place two webs side by side instead of spacing. It certainly doesn't give any more strength but does supply a bigger web area for the large coil springs to stand on.

Normally webbing is tacked on to the front rail first and stretched to the back and then from side to side. The anchor end of the webbing is turned over at least an inch and secured with five $\frac{5}{8}$ tacks in two rows of three and two. The other end is then taken up in the web strainer and stretched towards the back rail and secured by four tacks. It is then cut off leaving at least an inch to turn over and be fixed with a further two tacks. The turning over of the web acts as a kind of buffer against the tacks being driven home too hard, whereby the head of the tack can break off. Also as the tacks come from the mouth of the worker they can sometimes rust the material. The overlapped part takes any damage whilst the threads of the strained part are unimpaired. The practice of doubling over material after it is cut or trimmed around the frame applies to all material except the first-stuffing scrim and of course the actual covering material. Judging the right amount of tension in the webbing is largely a matter of experience, but a common practice is to let your hammer head fall from a loose wrist on to the strained web where the 'bounce' will denote if you at least have the minimum tightness. When webbing occasional chairs with delicate frames or loose seats then it is necessary to avoid buckling the frame by overstraining the webbing. Generally speaking, the backs and arms of chairs and settees do not require as tight a webbing base as the seats do.

Twines

Various grades and qualities of twine are used in the trade and also a variety of knots. Twine is first used (for the seat) in sewing in the springs, and this calls for a medium-thickness twine and, as for all other twines, one that will knot easily and tightly. We next go on to the lacing of the springs which calls for a 'lacing' cord which is a stouter twine altogether than any other that is used. It is called a laid cord. Twine plays a great part in upholstery and again it is used to stitch the top rungs of the springs on to the covering canvas and then to insert what are known as 'bridles' on the canvas. These are a series of loops running parallel with each other which hold the stuffing in place. The best-quality fine twine is used in the stitching of edges, covers, and for 'buttoning' or 'tufting'. An edge that is entirely stitched and not sprung usually consists of two 'blind' stitches and two 'top' stitches. A 'through' stitch or 'holding' tie is also used for holding stuffing in place after the first scrim is tacked on. Stitching or lacing of any kind always begins with a slip knot and it is a good rule to 'knot' whenever possible at all points held by twine. When lacing springs it is best to adopt one kind of knot and stick to it throughout. A sketch of probably the best type of knot for lacing is shown (p. 57.)

When at the stage of putting on materials, whether they be hessian, canvas or covers, do not be afraid to use temporary tacks until the adjustment to the right position is achieved. Temporary tacks are those that are only partly driven in and can be removed easily when satisfied that the covering is ready to be tacked right home.

Because fibres give a harder edge and are cheaper than hair they are generally used for first stuffing. Hair and black wool make good second stuffing. A calico covering over this makes a good job, and a final layer of wadding or linters felt completes stuffing prior to the cover going on.

The priorities in upholstering a piece of furniture like a settee or easy-chair differ very often according to the opinion of the upholsterers. The type of frame and springing also have a say in the priority of jobs and procedure. However, it is generally best to web and spring the arms and back first and bring to the first-stuffing stage. Then continue with the seat, bringing it also to the first-stuffing stage. As arms and back require more time and skill in fitting covers it is usually better to do them in that order, leaving the seat and the borders and facings until last.

In the following chapters the basic principles set out will be amplified further still, particularly as regards to webbing and lacing of the springs.

CHAPTER NINE

Webbing

THE webbing stretched across the frame can take the weight of three and sometimes four persons on a settee or perhaps just one person on a dining-chair. But no matter how many it can be readily appreciated that if a skimpy or a poor job is made at this, the first stage, any further work is wasted, despite how well it may be done. Well then, a good-quality webbing is essential, particularly if one is webbing a large area like a settee or easy-chair.

Unless it is a non-sprung job the webbing is attached to the underside of the base rails. Turn the chair or settee upside down with the arms resting on the trestles, or if this is too high a working position, leave it on the floor. Many upholsterers prefer webbing a job in this position. After deciding how many webs and what spacing, the webs are tacked on to the front rail to start and strained towards the back rail, using the basic method as described in chapter 8, i.e. overlapped ends, holding five tacks and the strained end being held by four tacks with a further two to fasten down the inch overlap allowed when cutting. In the case of a settee, however, the long webs for the length of the settee are tacked first with the webs from back to front interlacing over and under. It is this interlacing that gives great strength and springiness. Because of the extra length, settees have a stretcher rail across the centre from back to front to strengthen the frame. The strain on the webbing is apportioned more evenly if the webbing is tacked down across these stretcher rails. This is done by doubling a strip of webbing longways and tacking it over the webbed seat acting as an extra strapping. In the case of a long settee with two stretcher rails this gives three separate areas that take the weight independently.

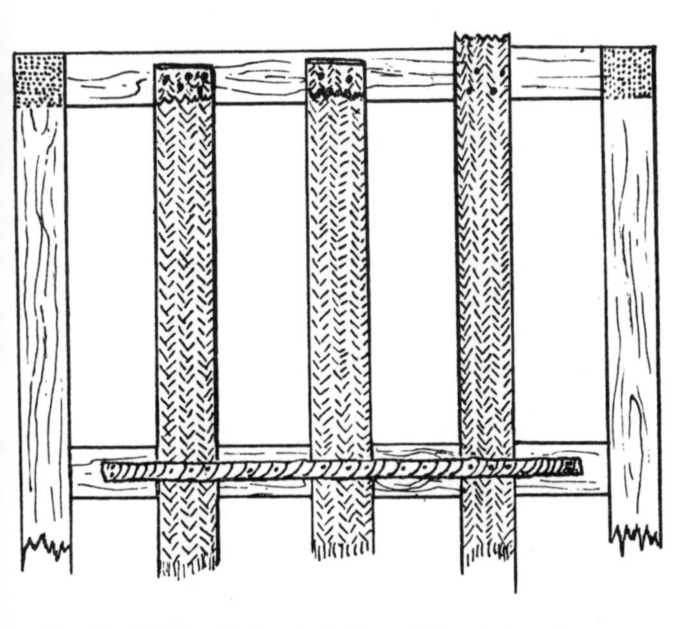

Fig. 13. Webbing finishes including additional strapping across stretcher rail.

The method of using the web strainers will be seen in the drawings (p.13). In the case of the simple strainer the rebated edge is placed against the frame at an angle of about 30 degrees. The webbing is brought over the gripping part and held there with the palm of the hand and, using a downward pressure, it is stretched to the required tautness. The lever type allows the webbing to be looped over the metal lever and held against the frame by the rebated end, the pressure being applied in the same way. The webbing is looped through the slot in the last model and held in position by the piece of dowelling or rod and again stretched by a downwards pressure. Seats and backs that are not to be sprung are webbed on the upper face and inner face of the foundation rails respectively.

How tight to strain webbing comes surprisingly quickly and after a little practice the 'feel' of the job is acquired. With a stout frame, a first tentative stretch is taken and then a fresh bite or pull on the webbing and a final stretch. It is at this point that the practice of testing the strain by allowing the hammer head to fall on to the web under pressure comes in, and by bounce and sound the experienced upholsterer can tell if it is stretched the correct amount. Nevertheless, when webbing dining-chairs, stools and loose seats or occasional chairs where the frames are smaller and often more delicate, great care should be taken, for if the straining is overdone it will buckle the frame. With this type of frame it means a complete reassembly, gluing and cramping, to regain proper balance or perfect fit in the case of loose seats.

The webs for the back of a chair or settee need not be quite so tightly strained. The back doesn't take anything like the weight that seat areas take. Also the arms which are webbed on the inside need only have them from the top of the arm rail to the bottom tacking rail. It is not necessary to have webbing lengthways. Very little stretch is required here for it merely acts as a firm foundation on to which a canvas and stuffing is upholstered. It also is a place where a lesser-grade web could be used without any danger of sag. Any springing of arms is done on top of the arm rail. The practice of springing the inside has fallen away, which is a good thing for it served little purpose.

Mention was made in the previous chapter of combination webbing, particularly on large areas. This is a method whereby two webs are placed side by side, a gap and then another two webs. This gives a bigger area for the usually large coil springs to stand and be sewn in. However, the evenly spaced method of webbing will usually meet all requirements and on balance is the best method.

When re-webbing a repair job it is essential that all the old tacks should be ripped out and any sharp ridges in the timber from this operation smoothed out with a rasp. Any friction caused by old tacks can help wear the webs.

CHAPTER TEN

Springing

THE hand-sprung job, particularly today, is a fair guide to good-quality upholstery. One could almost describe it as the bespoke part of the trade. This of course does not mean that other forms of springing don't produce good-quality furniture. Quite the opposite, in fact, for not only do the manufacturers turn out good-quality upholstery, they also combine it with excellent framework, particularly with show-wood settees and chairs.

However, in building a hand-sprung job the craftsman can make himself a foundation exactly to his design or liking and to match the type of upholstery he has in mind. The combining of different-size springs and different gauges gives a flexibility to the creation of the article. For not only does the springing give shape and body, it also decides the amount of 'give' to weight upon the different parts of the article.

After deciding how many springs are wanted for the seat and back, and sometimes the arms, together with the various gauges, the sewing-in of the springs can proceed. In the case of a seat they are placed upon the webbing and evenly spaced, the edges of the top coils being approximately two inches apart. A point to watch for here is to see that the 'knot' that finishes off the making of a spring is facing towards the centre of the area being sprung. This of course applies to the outside rows of springs mostly. When these 'knots' face outwards they are liable to tear the spring canvas that eventually covers the springing and is tacked down on to the bottom rail. In springing chair or settee backs the springs are usually placed a little farther towards the top rail which brings the bottom row just above the level of the seat. Also this bottom row of springs can sometimes be longer springs and a stouter gauge, depending on the design of the back.

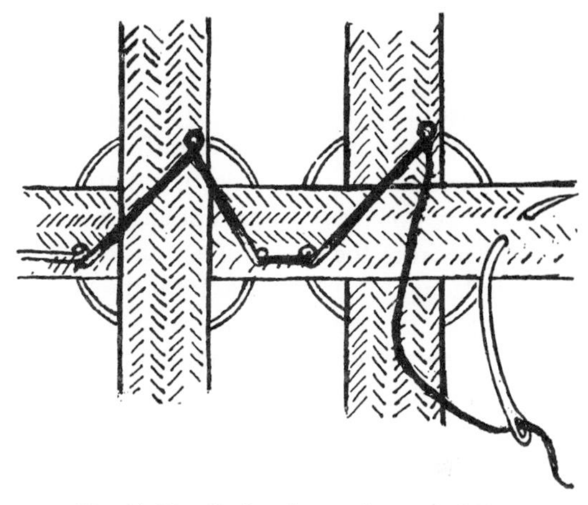

Fig. 14. Detail of spring sewing to webbing.

Having placed the springs in position the spring needle is threaded with a medium twine and the sewing-in started. At this stage upholsterers sometimes mark the webbing where the springs are standing and remove them from the webs, as they are usually knocked over in the process of sewing-in. They then place them one at a time as required. This is much easier and also allows you to start from the back of the farthest point away from yourself. The 'spring' needle, or 'packing' needle, is passed from underneath to come out close against the spiral coil and then returned on the other side of the coil and a slip knot tied, and pulled tightly, firmly holding the spring to the webbing. Each spring is caught at three points in this way, being tied with a single knot at each point and a double knot at the end or whenever the twine runs out. When the area is completely sewn in, the springs should be quite firm and unable to turn. They are now ready to be laced together with a laid cord. The object of lacing the springs together is threefold. It stops them moving about; it puts them under tension and they are tied or laced just in the right position. The springs on the perimeter when laced are leaning slightly outwards but with the compression of the springs when any weight is upon them, they compress to an upright position. The lacing is started from the back rail and tacked off at the front, and in lacing 'back' springs, from the bottom rail to the top rail. In the case of arms springs the procedure is from the inside to the facing, longways.

Assuming we are lacing the seat of an average easy-chair, there will likely be nine springs in three rows of three. Cut off three lengths of laid cord, the distance from back to front, and approximately half as much again. Fix three temporary tacks (tacks only half driven home) in the back rail in line with the centre of the spring row. Loop the cord once around the tack leaving a tail end long enough to reach the top coil of the spring and to knot it off, and then drive home the tack. With the three lengths of cord now anchored in this fashion, come to the front of the job to start lacing. Pass the cord around the third rung down of the back spring and pull back the spring until it is leaning towards the back rail. Hold it in position by the cord and then place the palm of your hand on top of the spring and compress it to a distance it will be likely to take when anyone sits on it. At this point of compression the spring should be upright and it is then secured by the knot as illustrated (*see* Fig. 7). From that position the cord is brought up inside the spring to the top spiral, knotted again and thence to the next spring. The centre springs of course need less tilting back and the spacing between the top knots of twine are about an inch apart or equal to the spacing on the webbing. As the front row of springs is reached, the procedure is reversed with that spring leaning towards the front and dropping the cord inside to the third rung down. The whole row of laced

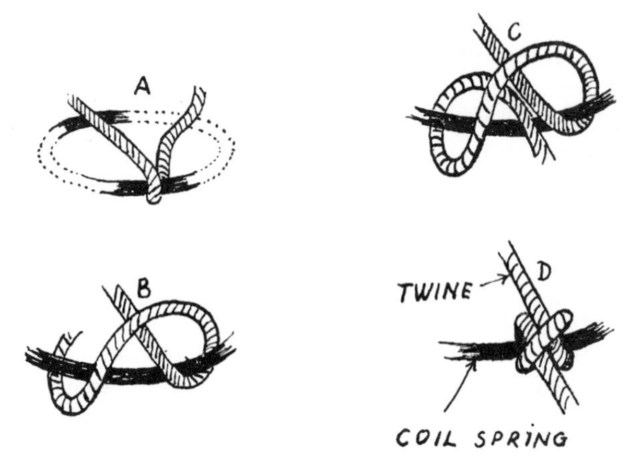

Fig. 15. Stages of lacing knot.

springs is then pulled taut and tacked home, the end of the cord being looped around the top coil and knotted. The ends of the back springs can all be done together after the completion of the lacing. The lacing from side to side serves the purpose of keeping the rows of springs straight with a slightly less bias towards the sides. As the laid cord crosses the long lacing from back to front, give a loop over the cord just to make a firm entity to the whole thing. It will now be seen that with any weight on the centre of the seat the whole spring foundation compresses but the springs revert to an upright position. This is the method of creating firm seating foundations that last for years and give lasting comfort. The springing is not allowed to buckle or twist and the maximum life is gained from the temper of the spring. The same basic operation applies to the other parts to be sprung but with a lighter touch. For example, back springing is carried out with lesser-gauge springs for softness. Every effort must be made to retain this softness. By putting too much tension on the springs or by too tight a lacing this softness can be lost.

The reader by now will be able to appreciate the tremendous difference in 'work time' between the hand-sprung job and the patent-sprung suite. The units of patent springing which have been decided upon, for size, number of layers, etc., are fixed in a few minutes by half a dozen clout nails driven through the holes in the steel webbings. Despite the fact that there is little variation in tension over the whole spring unit, the double layer minimizes the weight and distributes the pressure. Of course a good percentage of upholstered furniture still incorporates spring units for its springing foundation and it is very comfortable indeed.

Tensile springing

This is in the form of a cable spring (*see* Fig. 9) and also a rubber webbing. It was first used on fireside-type chairs and is now used for almost everything but the heavier-type suites. It is a most relaxing and comfortable springing used in conjunction with a foam-rubber cushion or a cushion with a pocketed spring interior. The side rails are built up to the correct height to take the cable springs which can be fixed in various ways.

One method is by inserting the hooked end of the spring into a 'grooved' side rail and driving a nail through from the top of the rail and through the hook. Another way is to fix metal plates on to rebated side rails. These plates have holes already bored at intervals to carry the hooks of the cable spring. Eyelets punched into a stout tape with a covering tape attached is yet another system of suspending this type of springing. This tape is nailed around the eyelet holes with a small-type nail. This form of springing is stretched across the side rails but a radial-type unit is available whereby the cables radiate from a centre boss to all four rails. The rubber-webbing type of springing can be fixed either from back to front or between the side rails and of course both ways together, interlacing as in normal webbing. This webbing is usually finished with right-angled metal clips on the ends which are held between a supplementary inside rail, and the chair frame.

The main difference in action between this type of springing and the coil spring type is the stretching of tensile springs against the compression of the older-type spiral spring.

Spring edging

I have left the skill of spring edging until last for this part of springing is a little more complex and should be studied separately. Almost every easy-chair and settee is now made with a spring edge and only the cheaper grades and pieces like dining-chairs or office chairs lack this type of edge. It is remarkable how many people sit on the edge of a chair in preference to the main body of the seat, but no matter where they eventually settle down the spring edging takes the initial brunt of the weight, and also gets probably forty per cent more wear than any other part of the seat. So it will be seen that this is a job that mustn't be skimped for time.

The springs used for edges are shorter and of a heavier gauge than those used in the main body of the seat. The principle remains the same, however. That is, when one sits on the edge, the springs will depress to an upright position. Firstly, tack a piece of felt or webbing on to the rail carrying the spring edge. This stops any noise against the timber when the coils hit the rail on depression. Place the springs in position and secure them with three or four staples. The bottom rungs may protrude over the edge rail in front; if so, hammer flat against the face of the rail. Each spring is now pulled forward towards the edge about ten degrees and fixed there. This is done by a length of webbing of half-width (approx. 1 in.) which is tacked against the front rail, left of centre of the spring, passed over the centre rung and the other end tacked off this time slightly right of centre (after the necessary 10 degrees tilt, of course). The whole row is treated in the same way, and is now ready to be pulled back to an upright position. A medium twine is used of sufficient length to come completely over the spring allowing for three knots. Tack these lengths of twine on the inside of the front rail and in line with the centre of the spring. Loop the twine around the centre rung and pull until the spring is almost vertical, knot and carry twine to top rung, knot and across the top of the spring to be hitched again and then taken down to front rail where it is tacked off. Every edge spring is treated thus. The next operation is the one that actually creates an even line and the means by which the covers and other materials are attached. This is the fixing of the cane on to the top rung of the springs. It should be long enough to go along the front and return around the end springs about 4 in. The thickness is about $\frac{3}{8}$ in. It is bent to return at the corners by notching the cane with a sharp knife and holding a flame under the notch, bending slowly. This will ensure that it doesn't break or splinter. The cane is now ready to be laced to the top rung of the springs with fine twine. Lengths of twine about 10 in. are doubled and looped over the cane and top rung. Hold the cane in position by attaching all the twines with a few loops and then complete the stringing. Each spring should have a length of looped twine of about 1 in. wrapped tightly around the top rung and cane. Tie off securely. To complete and make a firm job it was the habit to wipe the long knots over with the glue brush.

In the photo illustration (*see plate* 3) the webbings at the front are looped over the bottom rung but one. In this case the springs are short ones and it is the most suitable spiral to use. The supplementary rail to carry the spring edge is raised well above the base frame rail.

CHAPTER ELEVEN

Types of stitched edges and fronts

THE outside edges of upholstered furniture are usually made into a roll to give firmness and a smooth edge. The edge of a seat is normally called the 'front'. Edges are labelled 'stitched edge' and 'thumbroll' and in America the terms are 'stuffed roll' and 'cordroll'. When edges are required on the less expensive furniture the thumbroll is made, as it is one of the simplest forms of making a roll to soften the frame edges. A piece of spring canvas is cut off, the length of the required roll and about 4 in. wide. This is tacked on to the frame edge which has been prepared by rasping the sharpness away and leaving a narrow-angled edge, into which the tacks are driven. The tacks, five-eighths fine, pierce a double thickness of canvas, for this too has a hem, and are spaced closely about ¾ in. apart. The stuffing is then laid along the edge in an even thickness and the canvas rolled tightly over it and at the same time kept right on the edge of the frame. When it is rolled to the required thickness tack through the canvas on the inside and straight down into the rail again, keeping as close to the edge as possible without splintering the wood. Here again close tacking is needed. Start from the centre and proceed along each side in sections of about 4 in. at a time. If a tack is driven in about this distance whilst the canvas is being pulled by hand the intervening space can be filled without giving the roll a corrugated appearance caused by individual tack-draws (the strain where the tack is driven home). One soon gets the feel of how much stuffing to roll into the canvas. Remember the aim is to get a smooth firm edge without a bumpy finish which of course would show through the cover.

Black or ginger fibres make a good roll and also wool or the cheaper flock or wood-wool which makes for a nice hard edge. This might be desirable when doing leather-cloth covering jobs.

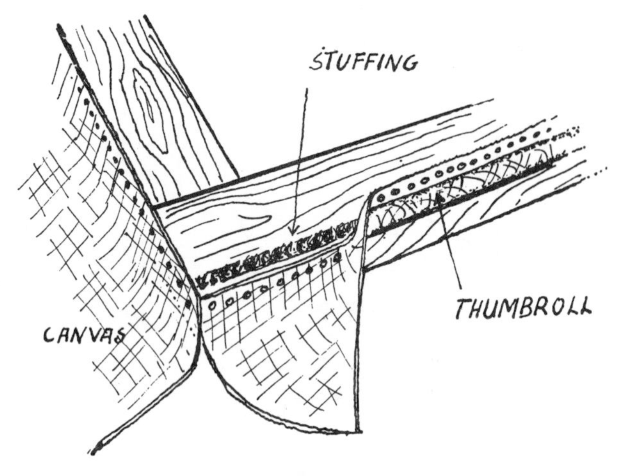

Fig. 16. Detail of a 'thumbroll' tacked on to a rasped edge of the wood.

The thumbroll is used mainly when the furniture calls only for a shallow stuffing and of course actually saves the task of doing a first stuffing. The height of the frame edge is invariably built up to compensate for the higher stitched edge that comes with a first stuffing.

The 'stitched edge' is achieved by regulating and stitching three or four rows of twine along the edge of the first stuffing. After the first hessian or scrim has been put over the fibre, or whatever stuffing is used, the 'front' or edge is built up to a level of the top of the springing. This of course applies to jobs without spring edges such as dining-chairs, etc., and any hard-edge seating. In the case of spring edges the first-stuffing scrim is brought over the cane edge and sewn on before a roll is stitched into it.

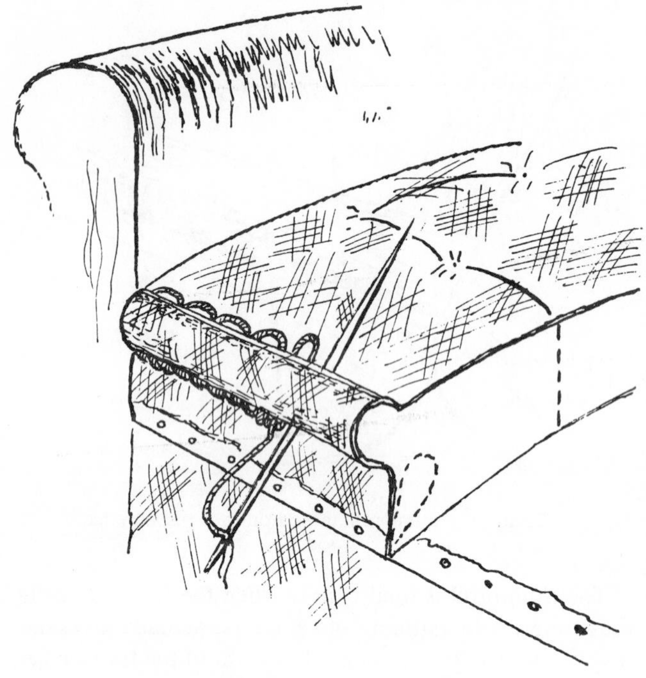

Fig. 17. Detail of stitched roll.

Assuming we are to stitch the edge of a dining-chair the 'scrim stuffing' is built up to the required level and the hessian turned in and closely tacked along the chair edge.

Using the 'Regulator' tool, the fibre is brought to the front evenly and the edge-to-be formed with the hand as you move along. With the four fingers on top of the hessian and the thumb slightly underneath forming the shape, it is surprising how sensitive and what an excellent guide the hand can be.

The stitching, which is done with an upholsterer's needle and fine twine, consists of two forms. The first is known as a 'blind stitch' and the other as a 'top stitch'. The former holds in position the stuffing brought forward by regulating. This is done by inserting the needle near the base of the stuffed edge, and pushing it well into the seat until it comes out on the top. The grip is changed to grasp the needle on top and to continue withdrawing it until the eye of the needle *almost* appears. It is then returned to the point about an inch farther along from the point of insertion, taken completely out and a slip knot tied and pulled tightly. Moving from left to right the needle is again inserted about an inch along and the procedure repeated but this time bringing the needle point out half-way between insertion point and last knot. As the point emerges loop the twine around the needle once and withdraw it. This forms a knot that is pulled tightly, again using the left hand to help form the shape. This is repeated until the whole length of the edge is completed. There will now be a row of stitching along the base of the stuffing but none showing on top, hence the term 'blind stitch'.

The regulator is once more brought into use, fetching the stuffing again forward ready to take the 'top stitch'. This is started at the same place and again with a slip knot but this time the needle is completely withdrawn when it emerges from the top of the seat and then inserted about $\frac{3}{8}$ in. back to come out about the same distance from the original entry point. Again moving from left to right the same process continues as with the blind stitch. Two differences are that the twine is shown on top and forms the 'roll' and a double hitch is made around the needle when forming the knot. This helps to keep the knot tighter. The insertion of the needle at the right point each time is important, for like the thumbroll the finished task must be even and without lumps. After the first stitch or two one is able to visualize the line the roll will take after pulling tight the knot. However, it will now be apparent what help can be gained in tacking the hessian along a thread line whenever possible. For instance along the front and back of the dining-chair. Of course some dining-chairs may require more than one 'blind' and one top stitch. An example could be a chair to be covered in hide. Now this will require a very firm edge mainly to withstand the pressure put upon it when covering it, and in this case two of each type of stitch is not unusual.

The same principle can be applied to an easy-chair without a spring edge. In fact the higher the finished edge the more stitches required to give it the necessary support. The sprung-edge furniture requires only a blind stitch and a fairly wide top stitch to give it a much more rounded roll.

The stitched edge can also be applied in a more economical way and is used extensively in American upholstery. Instead of a complete first stuffing all over the springs a border of burlap about 12 in. wide is sewn on to the canvas with a curved needle and twine, and then the edge built up in the same way. The burlap is sewn about 4 or 5 in. in from the edge. With jobs like bar seating already mentioned, it is tacked on to the wooden base, the edge stitched and a second stuffing bridled in ready for the cover, which is nearly always a good-quality leathercloth.

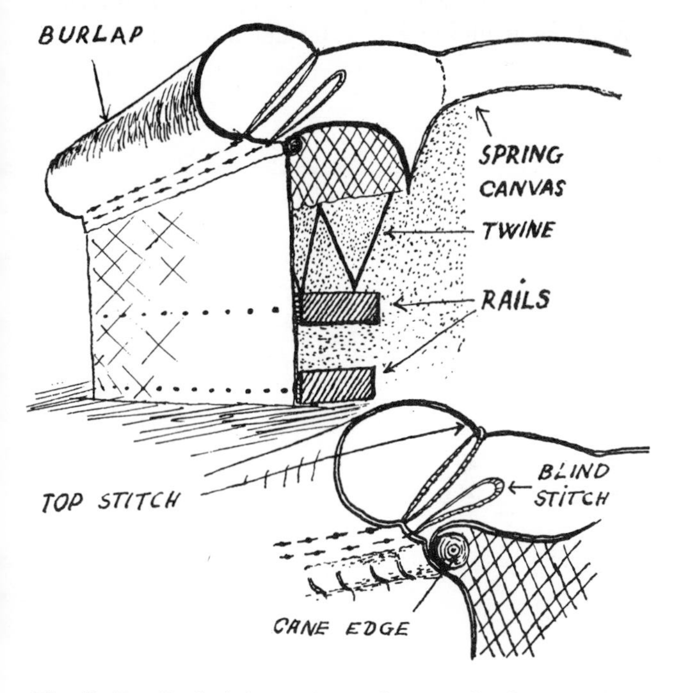

Fig. 18. Detail of stitches and guttering or gully, for a platform seat.

This is also an excellent method when a shallow seat is called for with a good edge. A very crude way of attaining a rounded edge is by nailing a piece of quarter-round wooden beading along the frame edge. Loose seats because of their shallowness of stuffing merely have the edges of the frame rasped 'round' the wadding covering giving it the softness required for the cover to go against.

The fibre group of stuffings give the firmest type of edges and are less costly than horse-hair which of course has all the qualities required for upholstery stuffing.

CHAPTER TWELVE

Making an easy-chair with cushion seat

Frame

ALTHOUGH frames do not come within the scope of the upholsterer an illustration (*see* Fig. 6) shows an average type of easy-chair of an orthodox style. This should not be too difficult to make if the reader thinks he would prefer to make his own frame or perhaps feels he would like to complete the whole of the chair himself. Birch or beech timber is preferable to construct a frame of this type. They are hardwoods and although they may be tough to work from they give a sound job when properly constructed. The 'softwoods' whilst being more manageable also have disadvantages. They are not suitable for dowelling which is without doubt the biggest drawback. And also the holding of the tacks cannot be guaranteed with a softwood frame.

The main seat and back rails are joined by means of dowels which should be $\frac{3}{8}$ in. diameter. At least three dowels each are required for the above main rails but four are better. Blocks or braces should be screwed into the corners to give additional strength. These blocks should also be glued when fixing them. Two or three dowels for the lesser rails and the tacking rails will do, with sometimes one and nailing. When all the rails have been cut and prepared, glue up and cramp. Do not start to do any upholstery work before it is well set.

This frame is designed for a cushion-finish seat and this is known as a 'platform seat', the main-body part of the seat being level after leaving the spring edge, as opposed to a more rounded or balloon-like finish to a non-cushion seat. The back will be sprung in the centre only with a stitched edge around its top border. There will be no springing in the arms but there will be a firm first and second stuffing with a stitched-up scroll facing.

In a preceding chapter it was said that there is a variety of ideas regarding the priorities of upholstering the different parts. In this case we shall start with the arms, continue to the back and lastly the seat. Each of these parts will be taken to the stage of scrim stuffing. After this is reached it can be a matter of choice as to how the second stuffing and covering of the parts is carried out. A preference for doing the seat first, followed by the arm and lastly the back, is justified by enabling one to finish tacking each of these covers completely. When it is pointed out that all the 'flys' are tacked on to the base foundation rails, the reason for doing the seat first becomes more clear. For not until the seat flys are tacked in place can the arm and back flys be completed. Of course if there is a preference for doing the covers in another order, then it only means that the flys are temporarily tacked up on the tacking rails, and after the seat is finished brought down and tacked home.

When the main parts or inside covers have been put on, the outside arms follow and then the outside back; the very last bit of tacking being a piece of black canvas or linen which covers the underside of the suite.

CHAPTER THIRTEEN

The arm

STRETCH three or four short webs across the arm opening vertically, and on the inside. These need not be stretched very tightly as they take little strain and are mainly to give a foundation to the arm stuffing. The web closest to the back should be set very close to the rail. A gap between the rail and webbing should not be more than 2 in. This is the web that will form the opening through which the cover fly of the inside back and the inside arm will pass, and, of course, any canvas covering of these parts that precedes the cover proper. At this point and

Fig. 19. Arm webs showing opening between arm upright and last web through which covers are brought.

before I leave the question of this 'gap', it might be mentioned that many upholsterers continue the arm stuffing right through to the back and prefer to leave the 'gap' for flys in a hole cut in the canvas covering the back springs. I have always considered this an untidy job and it certainly weakens the back canvas, particularly if it is a sprung back.

The webs are now covered with spring canvas or burlap. Cut off sufficient to give yourself a liberal hem. Start at the bottom inside rail and fold over about an inch of canvas and tack along, keeping the tacks in the centre of the rail thickness. Stretch up tightly by hand and tack to the top rail through the single thickness of canvas. Now hem and tack the short distance down the facing and at the opposite end where the 'gap' web is. Two straight cuts will be needed in line with the rails so that the canvas can pass through the gap and be tucked around the web until later, when it can be sewn with a piece of twine. Fold the top hem of the canvas now and tack. Webbings and canvas all of five-eighths tacks.

We now prepare to put our first stuffing on. The fibre needs to be held in position until the scrim covers it and this is accomplished by twine 'bridles', or loops. A packing or spring needle with a length of twine is used on the canvas part. Attach the twine at the bottom inside corner with a slip knot and from this point make large loops about 7 in. long and about 6 or 7 in. apart in parallel lines. The loop is made by inserting the needle and bringing it out again an inch backwards from the starting point. This is known as 'bridling'. On top of the wooden arm frame the same thing is done by using three-eighths tacks to hold the twine in position, remembering to leave sufficient room under the twine for the fibre to be placed.

The bridles on the canvas will give easily enough to pack under the stuffing.

The fibre can now be placed underneath these bridles and 'teased' or 'carded' out by hand evenly, to form the required thickness. Remember when using fibre or hair stuffings that there is a great deal of springiness in them, and although there may look adequate padding it soon compresses when the burlap is pulled over and tacked. So bolster the fibre well up into the bridles and press down with your hand to guide you as to the density. Bear in mind that where there is to be a stitched edge there should be no skimpiness, and see that the stuffing extends well over the edge of the framework. When the required density and evenness is obtained cut off the piece of burlap. Use a linen tape measure to get the size. When cutting canvas or any materials, it is a good rule to cut to a thread or wire. It keeps the rolls tidy and also ensures that you don't cut short.

Place the burlap over the arm and keep in position by temporary tacks, keeping the threads as straight as possible from back to front and from the top downwards. The 'holding' stitch or 'through tie' is now put in on the inside of the arm. This is needle and twine work again, and takes the form of two parallel lines of ties similar to bridles. Starting at the base of the inside arm pass the needle right through and out, returning it near the entry point and fastening off by making a slip knot. Moving along again in the same way as the bridling was done, pass the needle through about every 7 in. with the difference that the re-entry of the needle on top of the hessian is forward instead of back. When two rows have been done remove the needle and pull the whole length of twine tight, loop by loop, and tie off with a double hitch.

The scrim can now be tacked. This doesn't mean it can be tacked just as it is, for around the facing and along the outside of the arm you will find that it has to be built up to a firm shape, and this is done by tucking in extra fibre where necessary before turning in the scrim and tacking on the face of the rasped edge. When this is finished the scrim stuffing should overhang the edges slightly, for when you begin to stitch it will be pulled back almost in line with the frame. When finishing off the scrim at the back where the gap is, turn it in and sew it with twine to the edge of the web thus still leaving a free opening which the 'flys' will pass through. The tacks around the facing will not be more than half an inch apart, but along the bottom of the tacking rail and on the outside one inch spacing will be sufficient. Remember all edges of scrim will be turned under. We now have the foundation and general shape of the arm and it is ready to have the parts that take the weight or pressure reinforced as it were. In other words, the stitching. The edges along the top of the arm, particularly inside, take a lot of weight from the elbow which would soon disarrange the careful bridling of the fibre, if not stitched. Another place that takes a lot of pressure is the top edge of the facing. Most people place their hands at this point and take their weight both when about to sit and rise from the chair.

We start by regulating the stuffing to the front of the 'facing' edge using the left hand to form the shape. With a short upholsterer's needle put in a blind stitch all round the facing followed by a firm top stitch forming a roll along about the thickness of a hammer handle. Along the outside of the arm, regulate the stuffing and stitch in one blind stitch along the whole length, whilst on the inside a rather thicker roll is made at the point where it is desirable to maintain the roundness of the arm as it drops down to the seat. Before each stitching operation the use of the regulator is advised, for the more even the stuffing is formed before the twine goes in, the more successful will be your stitching.

At this point there is one arm completed to the 'scrim stuffing' stage. The other arm is now to do, and an important thing to remember is to make this arm identical in shape and size to the completed one. This has always got to be borne in mind when doing any stage of work on the arms of the facings. Once again, if the foundations are good the problems of matching diminish with each stage, as indeed do any other problems.

Just a word about stitching in a natural fashion. In the case of a right-handed person the stitching is done from left to right and therefore if the left-hand arm facing is done first the starting point will be on the outside of the scroll, whilst when stitching the opposite facing edge, the starting point will be at the bottom of the inside edge.

CHAPTER FOURTEEN

The back

As this is going to be a sprung back the webbing will be put on the outside of the rails. There will be four webs vertically and four across from side to side. The vertical webbing is to be done first and tacked on to the tacking rail of course and not taken down to the base rails. Anchor to the tacking rail first, using again five tacks for each web. It will be found helpful to rest something under this rail when tacking on the webbing to prevent 'springiness' when striking the tacks. And here is a rather belated tip regarding using web rolls. It will be found easier to use the outside end and the inside end of the webbing, and this will also give you two ends to work from at a time. Having anchored the vertical webs, stretch towards the top rail and secure with four tacks on each length. Cut off the roll, allowing an inch for hem, and the additional two tacks keep it down. The side webs are then stretched, not forgetting to interlace them. The frame should be on the floor, resting on its facings, during this job.

The webbing finished, the chair can go back on the trestles on its back ready to commence the springing. A spring layout for a chair of this type could be six springs of 6 in. × 12 gauge and three of 6 in. × 10 gauge. These will be suitable but there is no reason why more shouldn't be used but of a lighter gauge. There are some upholsterers who use the above number of springs with a modification of the lacing. They lightly lace through the centre rungs of the bottom row and the centre row whilst the top row is pulled towards the top rail with a twine anchored to the top rail, passed over the second and third rungs and returned to be tacked off. This method enables one to retain a softer back, the sewing of the springs to the canvas being considered sufficient to hold them in place considering the lesser strain on the back. However, there are others who prefer a softer spring and a full lacing as in the seat. Place the six 12-gauge springs at the top and centre and the three 10-gauge on the lower web. Sew in these springs in the same way as detailed in a previous chapter on springing, catching each coil three times and securing with a knot at each point. It is sometimes the practice to merely catch the springs to the webbing until they are all sewn in, and then tighten the whole length of twine and then knot it. This appears quite satisfactory when first done but with consequent wear it is surprising how loose the springs get. This naturally detracts from the sound foundation.

The springs are then laced fully but with a much lighter touch than when lacing a seat. The 'lean' of the top and bottom row springs is very slight. Tack the lacing cord on to the bottom tacking rail, allowing a return of twine to pull the top rung into place and proceed to lace the vertical rows. When ready to anchor the cord just take the strain but do not pull taut as in the seat springing. The side lacing is merely to keep the rows straight.

A piece of spring canvas or burlap is now tacked completely over the springing with a hem all round. Use needle and medium twine again to sew the canvas on to the top rungs of the springs. This is caught also at three points on each top rung and knotted. If one has chosen to lace only lightly as mentioned earlier then a little positioning of the springs may be necessary. This is done by just pushing them into place through the top of the canvas.

Now we are ready for the bridling, and this will require three or four vertical rows inserted in the same manner as for the arms. Two bridles along the top rail will also be needed. The fibre is worked under the bridles until the whole of the back is covered and a firm stuffing is achieved ready for the scrim. The base of the back should carry a little more fibre than the rest as a lot of pressure is put on there both when covering and also when in use. The stuffing should also be overlapping the edges particularly where stitching is to be done. The scrim is now tacked on with temporary tacks and the holding ties put in the centre of the back pulled tightly and tied off with a knot. The hessian can now be tacked off and will be started at the bottom rail, building it up by pushing extra stuffing underneath until it is at least stuffed out to the level of the springing. And the same applies to the sides. The hessian will pass through the 'gap' (the space between the rail and the last arm web) and be tacked against the face of the back rail. From the top of the arm and around to the other arm is built up in the same way for stitching the top edge. Remember to tack every half-inch and to shape this top border-to-be with the left hand whilst completing tacking the scrim.

Regulate right round the top border in preparation for stitching. In this instance there will be one blind stitch and two top stitches. When the edge is completed it should protrude past the level of the frame edge about an inch. This will make it almost level by the time a calico or cover is pulled over. The back is now completed to scrim-stuffing stage.

CHAPTER FIFTEEN

The seat

TURN over the chair and rest the arms upon the trestles ready for webbing the seat. Space out on the front rail the number of webs required, probably five or six, and anchor at this front rail using five tacks over the folded webbing. Stretch to the back as tightly as possible without buckling the frame or taking too much out of the webbing. Take the initial strain and then pull the web through the strainer a little farther ready for the second bite at it. The side webbings are interlaced and stretched across, finishing off in the same manner, four tacks with a further two to keep the hem down. The chair is then turned up to stand on the trestles ready for springing the seat.

Nine 10-in. springs by 8-gauge will serve for the seat. Here again personal choice comes into it. Some craftsmen would prefer to use six 10 × 8 and three 9 × 8, the latter being used in the back row. It is rarely a good scheme however to mix the size of springs. Like even spacing in webbing it is the unity that gives strength. Four springs are usually sufficient for the edge springing and the height of these will be governed by the front rail. If, for example, they are going directly on to the front rail then you will need an edge spring about 2 in. smaller than the main seat springs which would bring them about level with the seat. However, if there is a subsidiary front rail as in the photograph then a much smaller spring is needed. Most frames do have an extra rail for the spring edge, particularly if it is to be a deep seat. Place the main seat springs just by standing them on the webbing, starting with the front row, the position of which is governed by the distance from the edge springs. So hold an edge spring on the rail where it will eventually be stapled, and place the front row of springs about one inch behind the top rung of the edge spring. The rest of the springs can be placed and the webs marked or one can deal with them as the spring sewing proceeds. Do remember, however, to keep the 'wire knots' of the springs to the inside and so save the canvas from the danger of tearing. Sew in the springs in the same manner as described in the chapter on springing, i.e. every spring caught at three points and the twine hitched with a single knot until finished when it is tied off with a double knot. Then the lacing is carried out, starting from the back rail first and lacing towards the front rail. It is essential that the cord is tied well down the rungs of the front row, that is the last knot, and tacked on to the base rail and not, perhaps, on to the extra rail for the edge springs. The twine then does not interfere with the edge springs as they are depressed. The top rungs of the front row springs are pulled down with the end of the laid cord that was allowed before cutting. Complete the side lacings before starting on the spring edge.

The first job on the edge is to line the rail with a piece of felt or webbing to stop any noise as the rungs of the springs hit the woodwork. Staple the edge springs in position securely, for staples have a habit of springing out if they are on the short side, remembering again to keep the 'wire knots' on the inside. This is to ensure that an even line is kept when attaching the cane around the top rungs. The springs are now laced to assume their fixed position as described previously, by lacing from the back and over the top after the front lengths of webbing have pulled them forward slightly. Next notch the piece of cane

1. *Above:* This seat foundation shows clearly the outside springs sloping towards the corner and the technique of lacing. Another point to note is the outward slope of the stitched edge.

2. *Below:* Same frame from the other side showing the double top stitch and holding ties. The tacks seen along the front are driven home at an angle on the face of the rasped edge.

3. *Above:* This frame has a high step rail for the spring edge and consequently small springs were used. Note the piece of webbing along the rail to stop any noise when the spring is depressed. The cane makes a full return and is very securely tied.

4. *Below:* The hemmed canvas is plainly seen and the method of sewing the springs to canvas. The scrim stuffing has a roll stitched along the front, but it is not seen.

5. *Above:* This view shows the square-shaped facings and curved front legs. Note the stitch roll on the inside of the arm. The front of this chair will protude about two inches from the facings.

6. *Above:* Here are two stylish pieces of show-wood upholstered furniture by Greaves and Thomas, the seetee forming a single bed. The back and seat are fully sprung. The use of buttons helps break the long line as does the sectioning of the cover. Chair has a roll for resting the neck and the leg-rest slides out with slight pressure on the back.

7. *Above:* Another bed-settee by Greaves and Thomas. This one converts by foot pedal action to a double bed with its own interior-sprung mattress. The whole job is foam upholstered. The chair is similarly sprung and upholstered.

8. ***Below:*** A four-seater settee by Greaves and Thomas with special springing that blends in with the symmetry of modern furniture.

at the appropriate points and bend it by holding a flame under the notch, and attach this to the top rungs of the spring edge. Make a nice firm and neat job of this, keeping the cane in position and a constant height from the base rail. At this stage any discrepancies in lacing the edge springs will be shown up. For example, if one has been pulled down too far it will pull the level of the cane out of true.

With a tape, measure the amount of spring canvas needed to go from the back rail to the front rail, allowing at least six inches to go down between the main seat springs and the edge springs, to form a guttering. Also, of course, allow a little for hemming. Don't skimp this piece of canvas!

Fix on to the back rail with three or four temporary tacks and pull over the seat allowing it to hang over the front edge springs. A piece of cord is cut a little longer than the width of the seat. Anchor this with a tack just behind the facing and in line with the space between the main springs and the edge springs. Fetch the cord over the canvas to the other side rail, pull it tightly to form the gutter in the canvas and tack off, again on the base rail just behind the facing. Next throw back the piece of canvas lying over the front edge springs and, with a needle and twine and tacks, catch the cord forming the guttering and tack to front rail. In detail this is done by tacking a piece of twine at the left-hand side of the front rail, threading through a spring needle which passes through the underside of the canvas, catching the cord. The twine is then pulled to the front rail, missing the springs of course, and tacked. About three or four of these catches are required and they help to keep the guttering in position and form a firm separation between the main seat and edge springing. This then gives the independent spring edge. The spring canvas is now pulled taut and tacked off. You will find the scissors are required here to nick the corners where the rails meet in order to get any rucks or fullness out, although a pleat even might be necessary here and there. A pleated corner is necessary in front of the spring edge and this is slip-stitched with twine and generally a nice clean job made of this operation. When finished the canvas should be tight without having any effect on the lacing of the springs.

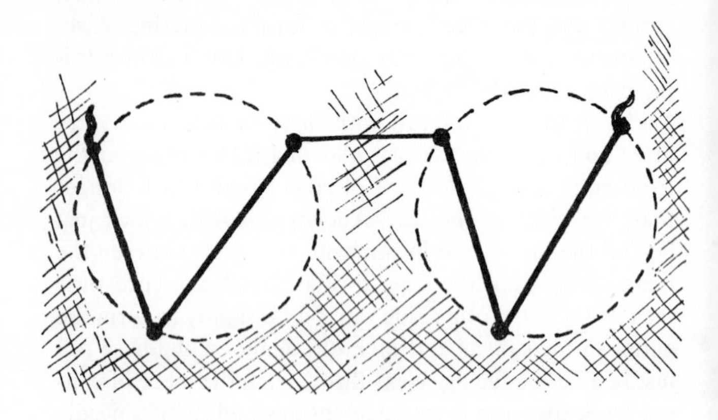

Fig. 20. Sewing top coil of springs to spring canvas.

The sewing of the springs to the canvas is now carried out, including the edge springs and the cane edge, which is caught about every inch along its length. The inside top rungs of the edge springs are connected to the top rungs of the front row springs by twine, bridging the gutter, but no tension is applied.

The foundation of the seating is now complete—a

foundation that will give comfort and stand up to almost any kind of treatment without breaking down. The twine bridles are now inserted in the same way as in the back and the stuffing commenced, the first job being to pack in the guttering. This is carried out firmly but without straining the ties between the springs. Here again an even stuffing is aimed at with the fibre overlapping the front edge and plenty in the inside corners of the seat. A piece of burlap is cut to cover from back to the front cane edge and placed in position. The centre of the seat has the necessary

Fig. 21. Scrim stuffing with holding ties and stitched roll at front edge.

holding ties and the back and side rails are tacked to the base rail, having first packed up with more fibre any places with insufficient stuffing. This mainly applies to the corners. The edge is built up ready for stitching in the same way, lifting the hessian and packing under any extra fibre required, tucking under the scrim and then keeping in position with a skewer. When the edge is ready for stitching the burlap is sewn on to the canvas and under the cane by the blind stitch, this blind stitch doing two jobs at a time. The roll formed should be about 1 in. in diameter. The important job of regulating applies here in the same way.

The chair is now complete to the first stuffing construction, usually described as 'scrim stuffing' stage. At this point if a three-piece suite were being made one would proceed with the other two pieces and bring them to the same state of readiness. This would be necessary in order to cut the covers as economically as possible. The next stage is to measure off the covers and to prepare them in readiness after the second stuffing has been applied.

9. *Above:* This ensemble by Greaves and Thomas has moulded plastic frames which are light and extremely strong. Foam upholstered with foam cushions. A pleasing and economical design.

CHAPTER SIXTEEN

Second stuffing—calico—covers

ALTHOUGH second stuffing can be covered with linters, felt or wadding and the covers pulled straight over, a more complete and satisfactory job is to cover the second stuffing with calico and then fix the cover over a layer of wadding. The calico covering has more than one advantage. In the first place it makes for a much cleaner job and has also the added advantage of keeping the stuffing in place if and when the covers have to be changed. As this chair is to have a single front border and the cover made in one piece, jacket style, it will be necessary to stuff up the border at this stage. Therefore insert bridles in the front border as well as on top of the seat and start to fill in the hair stuffing. Card it out as fine as possible as you build up to get an even surface and density. Not quite as much stuffing is required above the guttering for it is along this line that the hem formed by the lining and the cover that goes over the edge is sewn. Measure off a length of calico to go right over the seat and down to the base front rail. Pull this over the stuffing and temporarily tack. Once in position, a series of short holding ties in a straight line is inserted along a line over the guttering. The calico can now be tacked off to complete. Calico is neither hemmed or turned under but tacked through the single thickness and trimmed. In the same manner the second stuffing is applied to the arms and back and the calico tacked on. In tacking the back calico commence by tacking along the front of the 'tacking rail' and not right down on the base rail. The same thing applies to the arms, tacking the calico along the tacking rail. Where it meets the 'gap' it is sewn along the edge of the webbing. It will now be seen that the flys of the covers will be able to be tucked through to the main rails for tacking.

The cover can now be measured and prepared ready for putting on to the chair. It might be mentioned that this job can also be carried out at the completion of the scrim-stuffing stage and indeed would be if a calico covering weren't planned.

Covers

Figure 10 (*see page* 40) shows an approximate layout for the chair covers. If a complete suite were being done then of course each piece would be worked in to the best advantage. It is as well to check all measures before cutting, and also the cutting plan, paying particular attention to the matching pairs like arms and facings. Where a suite's covers are being cut, all pieces should be matched if possible, inside and outside backs and arms, seats and borders, etc. If it is a patterned material the main motif should appear in the identical places to get the perfect balanced effect. There will be eleven pieces to cut for the chair which consist of the outside back, inside back, the seat, two inside and outside arms, two borders, top and front, and two facings. Of these the seat, inside back and inside arms have certain parts to be machined before they are ready for tacking on to the frame. The remaining pieces like the outsides sometimes have pieces sewn on to make up the size. This is usually to economize with material.

Let us deal with the seat first. The measurements will

have been taken from the edge,[1] or rather just over the edge to an inch or so into the tuckaway (the space not seen where the seat, arms and back meet). This obviously will not reach down to the base rail for tacking, so pieces of hessian or canvas are sewn on to the back and sides. These are called 'flys' and after being cut they are pinned in position. The front border should be measured from just over the edge and down to the base rail plus 1 in. for tacking under. The length has to be long enough to return inwards at least 2 in. between the seat and inside arms. This border is sewn on with a piped edge to the seat and the ends joined up with the flys. It is necessary to mark the centre of the seat and the border so that they can be matched up when machining.

The inside back is now prepared. The measurements are taken in the same way but this time the cover must be skewered to the chair temporarily and the shape around the tops of the arms cut out. It is best to shape one side,[2] then fold the cover and cut the other side from the pattern made. Whilst the cover is still on the back, place the top border in position and make a small notch on the edge of the two pieces of cover, this will give a guide when it comes to sewing on. A fly extending from the shaped part is next attached but this should be made up from bits of the material for at least 2 in. from the main back piece. The border and flys are sewn on with a piped edge all the way round. Only the bottom fly is sewn on without piping.

The inside arm is measured from an inch around the back rail to an inch past the facing, and from under the

[1] Remember the seat covering will be made up from a lining material for the main part and about 4 in. or 5 in. of cover for the edge of the seat.

[2] A straight cut in the material will help in getting shape.

arm rail to an inch or so into the tuckaway where a fly is sewn on. Here again the arm should be temporarily fixed and pulled fairly tightly round the scroll of the facing. The material for the facings should be cut to correspond to the shape of the stitched edge and wooden facing, and a matching notch on to the arm cover made. This is necessary when the machinist is piping the two together. A long narrow piece to reach the bottom of the facing is joined on to the front edge of the arm cover where it enters the space between the front border and side of facing. The preparation for the second arm can be cut from the first providing the covers are back to back or face to face. Otherwise you will have two of one arm. This only leaves the outsides and if any piecing is to be done then the machining can be done all at one go.

In cutting shapes, etc., it is a good idea to make use of tailor's chalk for marking purposes. They can then be put flat on the bench and cut in comfort. Remember to allow three-eighths of an inch for seaming and piping.

We now start what is probably the most satisfying task in the whole job of upholstery. That of covering with the chosen material the finished upholstery. A lot of time was given no doubt to choosing the cover and one is always anxious to see just what the result will look like. This is the point where one leaves the dust, the colourless world of jute and stuffings and the hardness of coppered springs to commence the completion with an entirely new feeling. Whether the material be velour of the richest shade, or a moquette, or perhaps the sheer elegance of a silk damask. there seems to be an extra sensitivity to the hands as they mould and adjust the covers to their respective parts. To brush off any dust from the calico covering seems the most natural thing to do before putting the first cover on.

The seat cover is the first part to go on, and first a small twine-sewing job. The seam that is made, when the lining seat is sewn to the piece of material that covers the edge, is sewn along the line above the 'gutter'. This is carried out with a half-circular needle and fine twine. It is necessary to keep a straight line and such a guide can be pencilled on to the calico before starting. Where to mark this line is found by fitting the piped edge in place and noting how far into the seat the seam goes. When the sewing is done a single layer of wadding is put over the seat and the flys pushed down and temporarily tacked. Another layer of wadding over the edge and front border and again the cover brought over and a tack or two to hold it. Examine the sit of the cover at this point and see that everything is going to work out all right. In other words, note if any further padding is needed in any place and the cover is in the right position, etc. When satisfied, the cover can be tacked off, and this is done on to the base rails, on top of the rails in the case of the flys, and under in the tacking of the border. A small cut will be needed where the rails meet and the border is stretched around the seat sides making sure there is no fullness showing in front. The back cover jacket complete with top border is the next piece to go on. Once again a single layer of wadding covering the back and border and the jacket is pulled on. Adjust the shaped piping that goes around the arm into position and push down the flys. The first temporary tacks are for the side flys that go through the 'gap'. Pull these flys until the shaped piping fits snugly over the arm and then repeat at the other side. This sets the position and the next adjustment is at the top border. Here the piping has to sit along the roll formed by the stitched edge, and when this is set, a tack or two after straining the bottom fly will enable you to stand back and take stock of the job so far. If everything is satisfactory then any further stretching is done and the cover tacked off. In this case the back fly is tacked on to the base rail covering the seat fly, and the short arm flys against the upright back rail.

Before the inside arm and facing jackets are put on, there is still a small stuffing job to complete. The stitched scroll edge has only come down to approximately the level of the arm tacking rail, on the inside. It will be necessary to continue a thin thumbroll to the bottom of the facing where it meets the base rail. After doing this put a row of bridles in the facing and fill in with stuffing to give a padding to come level with projecting stitched edge. This is covered with a double layer of wadding and then the cover is pulled over. The piped facing is the first point to be set and here again the piping sits around the stitched edge. Tuck down the flys and temporary tack to check that it is sitting all right before completing. The fly is tacked to the base rail and the small piece of cover that comes through the gap after cutting where the rails meet is tacked against the back rail. The seam of the piping on the outside of the facing should just come around the edge to tack on the outside of the wood facing.

The outside arms are now put on, and we begin by back-tacking the cover to the underside of the main arm rail. Turn the chair over and rest the arms on the trestles. Lay the cover along the underside of the arm in position. Put a tack or two in to keep it in position. Next a piece of cardboard, the length of the arm by about ½ in. wide, is placed on the edge and back of the cover and then it is tacked along the whole length. This is tacked as near to the outside edge of the arm support as possible without splitting the wood. The cover which has been hanging to the floor, the back side facing you, is now brought over and tacked to the underside of the base rails and on the back of the upright back rail. Temporary tacks hold the cover in place down the outside of the facing until it can be slip-stitched later. It will be seen that the back-tacking makes a nice clean and strong anchorage without any tacks showing. The last piece of cover, the outside back, is now put on and tacked temporarily right round, only the bottom of the cover being tacked home on the underside of the base rail. The sides and top are slip-stitched at the same time as the arms. An alternative way is to use gimp pins and pin all round instead of sewing.

If the covering were a hide or a leathercloth, pieces of old material or canvas would be tacked in position first, before the outside covers were put on. This gives an added resistance against anything digging into the outside covers and tearing them. The protective pieces of canvas are termed 'linings' but must not be confused with the main cover. The American upholsterer in fact does call the outside covers 'linings'. Two more jobs remain to complete the chair. A piece of black hessian covers the bottom, and the cushion cover is fitted, which only means slipping the cover over whatever form of cushioning has been chosen and sewing up the mouth. If feathers or down has been preferred, then of course they will have been enclosed in a 'downproofed' case.

It might be mentioned here that piping can be of a more decorative nature by using a rouche. This type of finish does soften the whole line and takes away any severity the line of the chair may have. Be sure, however, that it goes with the cover.

CHAPTER SEVENTEEN

Pin-cushion seats—stools

MANY chairs, like bedroom chairs, occasional and office chairs, are lightly upholstered on the seat and always have a surround of wood. They are usually referred to as show-wood chairs, and the upholstery as pin-cushion seats. Sometimes one sees the backs also upholstered in a similar manner. Wherever this kind of seat or back is adopted, the main frame is slightly rebated in depth so that the completed upholstery comes level with the surrounding polished frame. The width of the actual tacking space on the rail is limited and one must be very careful when tacking, using the right-size tacks, which must be spaced evenly and as far away from the inside edge as possible without making a bulky rim against the rebated edge of the frame.

It is the simplest of upholstered seating, being just a stuffing over the foundation and a cover put on. No rolls are made and no stitching. As all the tacking is done on top of the chair frame it is necessary to first put on the black hessian bottom. This is tacked on with three-eighths tacks which are used for everything except the webbing where a half-inch-long tack is used. Two or three webs are stretched and interlaced each way. Extreme care must be taken when straining the webbing to ensure that the frame is not buckled or weakened in any way. Anchorage with four $\frac{1}{2}$-in. tacks is sufficient, with three at the opposite end; one tack being all that is needed to keep the hem down. These tacks should be in the middle of the tacking space, which will leave room for the cover tacks against the rebate. A piece of spring canvas is then put over the webs and a couple of rows of bridle loops stitched on the canvas top. Place the stuffing in position making a comparative shallow padding and 'tease' it out evenly. A double layer of wadding is then put over and the cover tacked on turning in the edges. (In the case of a leather cover no turning-in is required.) The cover is put on 'hand tight' but not so tight as to show the 'tack draws', i.e. where the strain of the tack makes a slight depression on the face of the cover. Temporary-tack the cover to check for pattern, straightness, etc., before finishing off. Soft covers are finished off with a gimp or braid which hides the tacked edge and also finishes off the job. Leather seats have a similar banding which is fixed with round-headed nails, of which there are various finishes. The gimp or braid can be put on with gimp pins or alternatively glued on. This is the type of upholstery that calls for the use of the 'cabriole' hammer with the small driving head. With the ordinary upholsterer's hammer the woodwork is almost certain to be bruised and damaged.

Stools

It is a fairly simple job to make an attractive dressing-table stool. Obviously the chosen style and dimensions would have to blend with the dressing-table, but whatever style is decided upon, the upholstering of it is very much the same. If you decide to make the frame then use a hardwood. Stools are rarely sprung, so consequently the webbing is done on top of the frame in the normal way and covered with a piece of spring, canvas. The edges of the rails should be rasped to take the sharpness off and leave a facet which tacks can be driven into. As the seat frame will be about 2 in. or 3 in. high a thumbroll is all that is necessary to form the edge. When cutting the canvas to cover the webbing, allow an extra 6 in. in length and width and let 3 in. overlap all round the frame. The canvas can be tacked on to the rasped edge closely and the extra 3 in. is used to fold over and make the thumb-roll. This is done in the manner described in chapter 11. A roll of about $\frac{3}{4}$ in. in diameter is thick enough, made as smooth as possible. Insert two rows of 'bridles' and fill in with stuffing. In this case fibre is suitable with a thin layer of hair on top. Cover with a piece of linters felt and tack a covering of calico over, making sure that the edge roll is clear of any pieces of stuffing. A layer of wadding precedes the cover which is tacked underneath, and then a gimp or fringe around the stool gives it a finish. A piece of black burlap underneath is optional.

The long footstool

Here is a piece of furniture that is years old in origin but still one of the most popular small pieces in the drawing-room. Its use, however, seems to have changed. Instead of a footrest one is more likely to see it covered with the current smart magazines laid out neatly, one overlapping the other. Nevertheless they are attractive pieces in the furnishing of the sitting-room. The length of these stools varies between 3 ft. 6 in. and 4 ft. Some of the older types can be seen with loose seats covered in gros-point material. This is very suitable covering and in keeping with the period. Another popular cover is a hand-worked tapestry. The frame can be made out of almost any kind of timber, a simple rectangular frame with four legs screwed on through the top of the frame. An alternative, and very popular, is six short cabriole legs that help to relieve the severe long lines of the frame. Glue and cramp the frame together and cover the top with a piece of ply or laminated wood. Rasp the edges and tack a 3-in. strip of canvas all round. Lay along the edge some flock or wool and make an ordinary thumbroll about an inch in diameter. Tack two rows of twine bridles along the wooden top and work in the stuffing. Black wool or even rag flock is suitable for a job such as this. Stuff rather firmly and cover with a piece of calico ready for the final cover. If a tapestry or a gros-point cover is used it is better to sew on a linen border around the top panel. This focuses the cover design and also gives height to the stool. A black burlap bottom completes the job that will give great pleasure to the skilled upholsterer or the amateur.

10. *Below:* 'The Gavotte suite' by Parker-Knoll. This firm has one of the greatest reputations in chair-making and manufactures some of the most comfortable and graceful seating arrangements today. This suite is made with walnut, beech, and mahogany frames and has a foam-cushion seat.

CHAPTER EIGHTEEN

Dining-chairs—loose seats

ONE of the most popular types of dining-chair is that of the loose seat variety. Although the period and styles varied they retained one thing in common, a framework within the chair seat that can be lifted out. Still produced in volume, they are extremely economical in material and the covers can easily be changed without incurring heavy labour costs. The loose seat frame is made of birch or beech and assembled by dowels or mortised and tenoned joints. Dowelling is the system most used today. The top side of the loose seat frame is chamfered so that the edge of the chair frame and seat frame are level. Make sure that it is a good fit before upholstering. It should have just enough play to take the thickness of cover. Plane a little off if you think it is too tight, and if too slack a piece of cardboard or webbing is tacked against the side or back and if necessary both. The average loose seat will take three webs back to front and two across the width. The tacking of the webbing should not extend beyond the line where the chamfer begins. It is strained in the normal way but again with great care to ensure the frame isn't buckled and twisted. The following spring canvas is tacked on in the usual way with a hem on top. The bridles are then sewn around the frame canvas ready for the stuffing to be 'bridled in'. Hair or wool are suitable stuffings but the former is preferred for it is the resilience of the hair alone that will help keep the shape of the seat and avoid that hollow in the centre after use. The stuffing should be built up high in the centre and covered with a piece of calico, and tacked with three-eighths tacks on the outside of the frame. This is trimmed to within a quarter-inch of the tacks. Care should be taken when doing this to keep the edge of the frame quite clear from stuffing. The seat should now be the required depth and quite firm. The cover, which needs no preparation, is cut off allowing

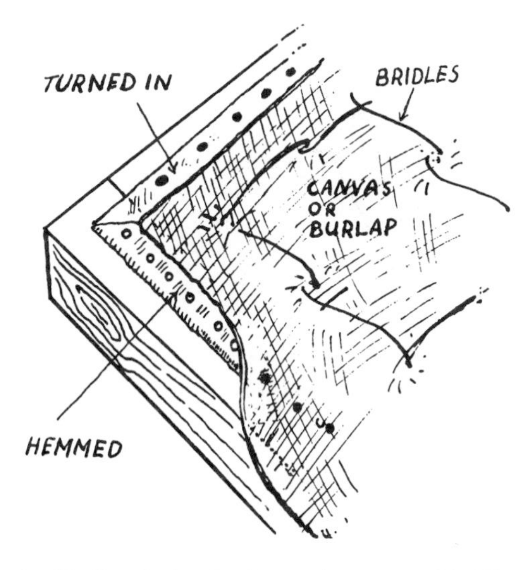

Fig. 22. Sketch showing hemmed canvas and bridles.

about an inch more than the net measurements. If the cover has a large motif in design it should be placed in the centre of the seat. If it is a pile material then the pile should run from the back of the seat to the front. Fold the cover lengthways and cut a small nick across the folded corner. This will serve as your centre guide to a similar mark in centre of the front rail. Lay the cover face down on the bench and place the seat on top, stuffed side on the cover. Fold over the front edge of the cover and fix with four temporary tacks. Turn over the seat and place a layer of wadding over the calico and stretch to the back holding the cover with a few tacks, and the same with the sides. Check that the pattern is central and satisfactory before tacking off. This is done in the same order, back to front and then the sides, tacking about every inch. The corners are turned in neatly at the very end of the rail as the illustration shows. A piece of black hessian or linen is tacked on the bottom to complete the seat.

It is not surprising that this type of seat is so popular for it is compact with a nice clean finish and easy to keep clean. Many of these loose seat frames have a covering of plywood instead of webbing foundation and while this makes the job less costly it certainly isn't as comfortable and does compress the stuffing very quickly, no matter what type is used. A more modern, efficient and comfortable seat is now manufactured with rubber webs and a foam-rubber stuffing. This certainly produces a clean first-class job.

Stuff-over chairs

The small stuff-over chair can be sprung or made with the firm seat. Dining-chairs that are sprung are of the modern variety whilst the period chairs such as the Chippendale, Hepplewhite and Sheraton depend for their comfort on hair-stuffed seats expertly upholstered. There was a time when nearly all small chairs of the dining type were made without any springing, but included in this chapter is a detail for springing such a chair, for those who prefer a sprung seat. Once the foundation is laid the method of stuffing remains the same. If a chair is to be stuffed, only then the webbing is done on top of the seat rail. If it is to be a sprung seat then it is webbed from the underside of the rail. Therefore to start the spring seat turn the frame upside down on the trestles and commence webbing. Best English webbing should be used for this with a combination usually of four long webs and three across the width, remembering to inter-lace them. Web from front to back first in the manner prescribed and again beware of overstretching and twisting the frame.

Although a small seat can be sprung adequately with three springs, it is nearly always better to use a five-spring plan. This is one centre spring with four surrounding it. These are sewn in with three ties to each spring in a triangle shape but need not be knotted at each point as in larger pieces of upholstery. After the first slip-knot the springs are caught with a continuous twine which can be tightened after the last spring is tied and then knotted. An average chair spring would be a six inch by ten gauge. The lacing of the springs tends to harden the seat a little and many upholsterers prefer to omit lacing and secure the springs by sewing them directly to the covering spring canvas. The springs are pushed into position through the top of the canvas, the outside ones leaning slightly towards the corners and the centre spring remaining upright. However, lacing is more dependable and this is carried out diagonally. As the twines cross only on the rung of the centre spring it is knotted. The finish of the lacing is done in the same way as the easy-chair seat with an end of twine tying off the top rungs. I feel the lacing is a much more satisfactory job. If necessary use a lighter gauge to retain the softness aimed for.

The spring canvas is put on and hand stretched until taut and then the tops of the springs are sewn on to the canvas. Bridles are then put in near the edge and across the centre of the seat. The fibre is 'bridled' in and the hessian put on, being held with temporary tacks and holding ties. The latter usually form a square shape in the centre of the seat.

Commencing with the front edge, first build up the stuffing to a well-filled edge and tack off the scrim, keeping the half-inch tacks along the same row of threads in the scrim along front and back edges. This will help you when you come to stitching the edge. Build up and tack the edge all the way round. When all the scrim is tacked the stuffed seat should be about an inch bigger than the frame size all round, for when the stitching is completed it will have pulled it in again. The 'regulator' comes into action first, bringing the stuffing near the lower part of the scrim ready for the first blind stitch. Start at the side, low down near the tacking, by pushing the needle well into the stuffing and returning it near the entry point to make a slip knot. From this point insert the needle about 1½ in. to the right, taking it well into the stuffing, but not out, and return it about half-way from the point of entry. Twist the twine around the needle as it comes out and pull the twine tight. Continue the procedure right round the seat. After further regulating, the second and third stitches are put in. These will be top stitches where the needle is taken right out of the hessian and returned, but a double twist is put around the needle as it comes out, making a tighter knot. During the stitching of the roll concentrate on getting a nice straight and even edge of equal height all round. The use of the left hand to help form the stuffing whilst regulating helps greatly. Because of the pulling of the twine after each stitch the top of the little finger on the outside can become very sore and even cut the skin. A safeguard is to put a leather 'stall' over the little finger. I have mentioned doing two top stitches but in fact one could do in the case of a soft-cover job. However, if hide or leathercloth is to be used as the covering then two stitches are certainly necessary.

The bridles are put in ready for the second stuffing which is laid evenly over, and then a calico cover tacked on. Where the stuffing is wool the calico is seldom used but the cover put on over a layer of linters felt or wadding. The cover is tacked on temporarily beginning by a straight front and after checking positioning, etc. The cover is cut at the junction of the back rails and at the front corners and folded to make a flat neat pleat on the front. Where the cover goes over the side and back rails it is turned in and pulled tightly downwards and close against the long back rails or uprights. After stretching the cover towards the corner it is continued around the front and a couple of tacks are put in about half an inch from the corner to hold it. Cut upwards along the line of these two tacks till near the top. The cover will then extend past the corner of the front border about 2 in. Cut off about three-quarters of this, leaving enough to turn in and make a neat pleat right on the corner. Unless this surplus is cut off it makes for a bulky corner which also can make a line on the cover later on.

Depending upon the style of the frame the covering is either tacked underneath or against a rebated frame, the lower part probably being polished. In the latter a gimp or banding is put round to finish off. Another finishing style is close-nailing with the round-headed nails. Chippendale-style chairs often have this finish and larger and older period chairs sometimes have extra-large studs.

The black hessian bottom is tacked on to complete a very satisfactory job.

The same procedure exactly is used for all stages when making a chair that has not a spring seat. The only difference being the webbing, which is done on top of the seat rail instead of on the bottom.

11. *Above:* This is the easy-chair on the Gavotte suite.

CHAPTER NINETEEN

Cable springing and latex cushions

CABLE or tension springing has become very popular in the last few years, particularly for the smaller type of chair and indeed for the well-designed easy-chair. The cable spring in appearance is the same as those fixed to 'exercisers' and sold in sports shops. They are made in various diameters and are usually covered with plastic, and in some cases with a material. The less expensive chair carries a spring without any covering at all. These cable springs are fixed to the side rails of the chair which are higher than usual and the inside of the rail is grooved or rebated. This is done to fix the springs as the sketches will show (*see* Fig. 9). Sometimes the hook of the spring is inserted into the groove and a nail driven through from the top of the rail, passing through the hook and groove before being embedded in the lower part of the rail.

Another method is to have metal plates with holes bored in at intervals screwed on to the side rails. The cable springs are then looped into the holes. This is an improvement on the grooved idea but this too can have a drawback inasmuch as the metal edge sometimes wears the cover. Perhaps the best type of fixing is the webbed tape idea. This is a double tape about 1½ in. wide and sewn together along one edge only. The under tape has eyelets punched in at intervals to carry the hooks whilst the top tape covers them and makes a neat finish. These tapes are fixed to the rebated edge of the frame by tacking with fine nails around the rim of the eyelets.

This type of seat- or back-springing was first used in conjunction with the spring-pocketed units in cushions. These consisted of light calibre springs sewn in individual pockets of calico or hessian and the whole assembly wired or clipped together making the complete springing unit. The unit is then covered with prefabricated stuffing and linters felt and sewn inside a calico casing. This form of seating cuts out a lot of work in the manufacture of a chair whilst providing a most comfortable seating foundation. Using the same principle of seating, another very satisfactory form of springing is by using tensile rubber webbing and latex cushioning. The rubber webbing is fixed to the side rails and sometimes interlaced in the same way as conventional webbing. It is fixed by nailing and some manufacturers fix a right-angled clip at the end of the web. This is kept in place by screwing an extra inside rail to the existing rails of the chair. Of course the better-class chair uses a latex cushion interior which is moulded to its particular shape and size of seat. Latex along with rubberized stuffing is undoubtedly an improved form of upholstery for many things and certainly makes the upholsterer's work easier and cleaner, without any loss of quality in the finished article. Of course there are many people who prefer the spring-interior cushion. The required type and size unit is bought and put into a calico case or it can be covered with rubberized hair and a layer of linters felt or wadding. Both sides of the cushion unit and the borders should be 'bridled' and the stuffing put under evenly. It is then covered with the linters felt or wadding ready for the actual cushion case. To get the prepared unit into the case one requires two pieces of ply or hardboard slightly less in dimensions than the cushion size. With one piece of ply on the bench lay on the prepared unit and place the other board on top. Pass two lengths of twine lengthways around the two pieces of board and with a slip knot pull tight and secure. It is now a simple job to pull the cover over, starting at the narrowest end of course. Once the unit is in the cover the twines are released and withdrawn along with the boards. A corner or two may need to be stuffed out before sewing up the cushion case. With a latex-rubber interior it is simple to fold it and slip it into the cushion case. It is always advisable to cover the actual rubber with a calico case first.

The finished cushion can lie directly on the rubber webbed type of seat, but with the cable-sprung job a covering of some kind is normally put over the springing. The chair that simply has four or five cable springs between the front and back rails has a lining hemmed at the sides and a pocket at each end through which the first and last spring is inserted respectively. Many cable-sprung chairs have the front rail set in at the lowest point into the side rails which enables two or three cable springs to be fixed closely together to form a spring edge. With this seat a separate piece of cover is hemmed at the width of the edge having sufficient length to be back-tacked on the inside front rail and brought over the combination of springs and tacked off under the front rail. The remaining main seat springs are covered with lining.

When sewing the lining for the seat the hemming is done first and then the slots are machined in. The lining is held only by the front and back slots and of course the whole lot goes down as anyone sits upon the chair, without any strain on the lining cover.

Most firms have machines for cushion filling with spring units but of course the general upholsterer rarely needs such a machine.

CHAPTER TWENTY

Bedding

Divan base

DIVAN bases are made in standard lengths and widths, i.e. 6 ft. 2 in. × 3 ft., 3 ft. 6 in., 4 ft. and 4 ft. 6 in. widths. Frames can be made from any kind of timber but are usually in a softwood. The normal dimensions for the sides and the ends are 5 in. × 1 in., and for the slates 3½ in. to 4 in. × 1 in. It is assembled by butting the ends to the sides, gluing and nailing. Strengthening blocks are put in each corner and a wooden bracket against the centre slat and side. Seven to eight slats are needed for a 4 ft. 6 in. base, which are inserted on the base rails at regular intervals. Pieces are cut out of the main rail the width and depth of the slat and the slats are set in and nailed. Make sure the frame is square (using the term as applied to a right angle of 90 degrees), before starting on the slats. Corner legs are then added.

The slats are first covered by a material to stop the noise of the rungs hitting the timber when depressed. This is usually a piece of webbing, canvas or felt. If a shallow base is required then 5 in. springs will be high enough, but the average divan requires springs of 6 or 7 in. by a twelve gauge. A 3 ft. wide base will take four or five springs per slat and a 4 ft. 6 in. base six to seven springs on every slat. The springs are stapled in with four staples for each spring over the rung and through the covering on the timber. They should be spaced out evenly along the slat, once again remembering to keep the wire knots of the outside springs facing inwards. The springs are laced lengthways first, so the number of pieces of laid cord are cut off for this job. They should each be the length of the divan plus an allowance for knotting each spring and an extra foot over at each end. This is required for holding the centre rung and tying off. Anchor each piece of laid cord in a line centre to a long row. This is best done with

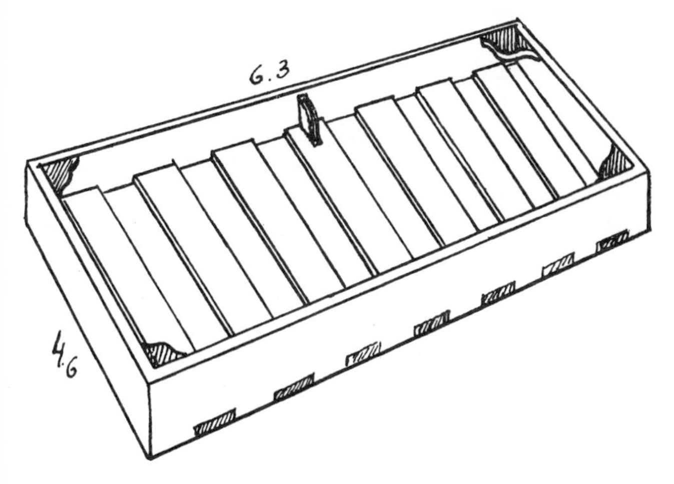

Fig. 23. Divan base frame.

a staple, leaving a foot of twine for finishing off. Commence lacing, tying off the springs as already explained, but starting directly on to the top rung of the first spring and not the centre rung as when doing a seat. The centre rung is caught with the end piece of laid cord and pulled towards the rail when the lacing is completed. Pull the cord taut after each row of lacing is done and secure with a staple. The lacing across the width is done in exactly the same way, not forgetting to cross the cord as it meets in the centre of the rungs. A piece of heavy-grade spring canvas, normally termed tarpaulin, is cut off 6 in. longer and wider than required to cover the springs. This is put over the springs allowing an overlap of 3 in. over the sides and ends. Tack every inch all round with five-eighths tacks, through the single thickness. The overlap is required to make a thumbroll with wool or fibre. Starting in the middle of any side or end, lay some stuffing along the edge and fold the canvas over tightly forming a roll about 1½ in. in diameter. Pull it well back to the edge and tack off every inch with five-eighths tacks. The aim is to get the whole length of the thumbroll as even as possible in thickness and without any lumpiness. The springs are then sewn to the canvas catching each rung three times. Because there is such a large laced area it is sometimes considered unnecessary to sew in the springs, and up to a point this is quite true. However, after use the canvas does stretch and lose some tautness and this does mean there is more play and therefore more friction from the moving canvas which results in wear over the top rungs of the springs, particularly where it catches the 'wire knots' of the springs.

The twine 'bridles' are then sewn in over the canvas top and the stuffing put under them, 'teasing' it out evenly as each handful is put in. The centre of the divan base usually calls for a little extra stuffing just to give it an extra inch in height. When the stuffing is completed a hessian covering is put over and pulled tight and tacked against the sides of the ends and long rails. The 'ticking' cover can now be cut off and prepared. Measure off a 'tight' measure over the hessian and allow half an inch for seaming. Make up the required area of ticking on the bench (it will probably need a full width with two part-widths on either side of it) and also cut off the separate border lengths and piping lengths required. The cover is then machined up with a piped border and a double stitching up the corners where the borders are joined. Before leaving the machine make sure there are no gaps in the piping, for a lot of strain is put upon the cover. Incidentally, the border lengths are cut to the depth of the divan plus half an inch for seaming and an inch for turning under and tacking. Pull the ticking cover over the hessian and temporary-tack all round getting the piped edge of the ticking in line over the edge of the thumbroll. When satisfied tack off underneath. The divan is now ready for tufting. The tufting takes the place of holding ties on the scrim stuffing. Mark out the top of the cover for as many rows of 'tufts' as required, which might be five rows of four, or three rows of four, interspaced by two staggered rows of three. When the cover has been marked, thread a long needle with fine high-quality grade twine and start to put in the slip knots through the marked spots. The knots are the things that actually hold the tufts which can be made of wool, cotton, leather and even buttons. Insert the needle from the top (at this stage the divan is standing on trestles at each end, allowing free movement in locating the needle as it comes through from the top) and pull it from underneath until it is through the spring canvas and then push it back as close as possible to the entry point. Make a slip knot and pull not too tightly at this stage, and clip off the twine leaving an end of about 5 or 6 in. Repeat this procedure until all the marks have been covered before putting the tufts underneath the twine. When all the tufts are in, commence pulling the slip knots tight and knotting off with the end of twine left on for this purpose. Cut surplus twine as near the knot as possible and tuck under the tuft. The tightening of the tufts is started from the centre working outwards each way. This particular type of divan base is now completed except for the tacking-on of a black hessian on the underside which keeps out the dust and finishes off the job.

The box mattress is made very much the same way as a divan base. This is the mattress that fits over the old-type bed irons. It has a retaining rail that is set back about 2 in. from the side and end main rails, and fits in between the bed irons. It is not unusual to find these mattresses webbed instead of having wooden slats for the springing to rest upon, and also made with a spring edge along the sides or at least with a stitched border. Of course when this type of box mattress is used it serves as a complete unit that doesn't need a spring-interior mattress over the top, although a pillow-type wool overlay is very frequently used. This is a mattress without a border, therefore quite shallow but giving that extra softness that might be required. There are better-quality divan bases that are made with spring edges all round but more often with the two sides and the foot only. Wheel attachments or good-quality ball-bearing castors make it much easier to manipulate the bed for making-up or cleaning purposes.

Sometimes the divan base is made in two parts and hinged to enable it to be folded in the centre. It can be space-saving and is easier for one person to move. Another popular adaptation, particularly with the single divan, is to put a blanket drawer in the base of the frame. This entails making a higher rail and using a shallower spring for the foundation.

Spring-interior mattress

As its name implies, this is a mattress in which the interior has springing of one kind or another. Various types of spring units are obtainable as described in the chapter on springing, such as the open-mesh type in which the small coil springs are joined by spring wire and the pocketed type where the springs are pocketed in calico casings and are clipped together. The first method has a hessian covering. The stuffings are varied from linters felt to all-hair. The last-named, of course, is always a first-quality job and in the highest price bracket. However, wool stuffing is greatly used and is a most satisfactory type of stuffing for a mattress of this type. The ticking case is made and will include handles, two on each side for lifting, and wire-mesh air vents in the borders. It should be remembered that a good-quality ticking is needed if a hair stuffing is to be used. A full-size mattress, i.e. 6 ft. 2 in. × 4 ft. 6 in., will be cut 6 ft. 5 in. × 4 ft. 8 in. The extra material is taken up by seaming and tufting. The borders will run out at 6¾ in. to finish 6 in. in depth after piping. The case is stitched around completely on one panel but only along one long side of the other panel. This leaves the ticking open to enable the spring unit to be laid in after the stuffing has been bridled around it. The panel is then pulled over and the edges skewered together to hold them until the ends and side are sewn together. Mark out the tufting spots (if they already haven't been done) and tuft, using first-quality twine. On a full-size mattress they are usually staggered in rows of four and three, looking across the width, and five with four lengthways. Put in all the tufts before tying off tightly, starting from the centre and working outwards. After the tufting is completed two rows of tying stitches are put right round the borders to retain the stuffing on the edge of the mattress and so keep the edge firm. This is done with a fine mattress twine and a long needle. After regulating the stuffing to the edge, start off about a third of the way down the border from the piped edge and make a slip knot. Don't bring the needle out on top of the ticking. Insert the needle again at almost the same point and return it about two inches farther along

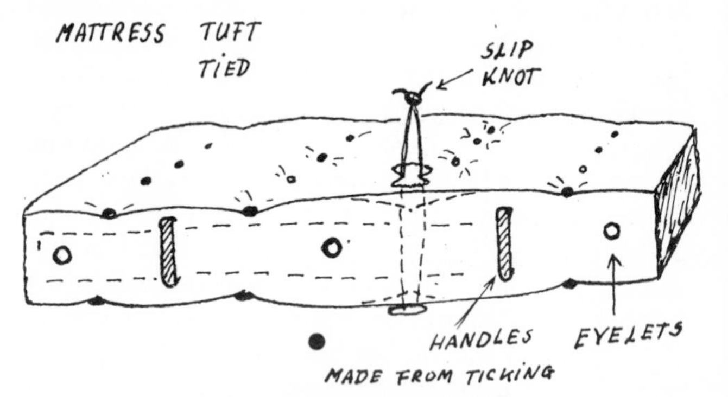

Fig. 24. Tufting a spring interior.

the border. Insert the needle again about a quarter-inch along the border and repeat until two rows have been done all round the borders. There is no twisting of the twine over the needle as in doing a blind or top stitch.

The manufacturing mattress-makers of course have machines to carry out many of these tasks and the above procedure applies to the smaller workshop. A great many spring-interior mattresses now have the borders reinforced and supported by quilting.

Latex foam-rubber mattresses are very popular and as

processing costs become cheaper a greater volume is demanded. They are made in thicknesses of 4 and 6 in. and will last a lifetime. Among the many advantages they have, constant resilience is a most important one along with the obvious hygienic properties.

Not all people like a soft or springy mattress and there are still a great number of 'hard mattresses' supplied. They are termed 'hard' as opposed to spring mattresses, although a 'stuffed' mattress might be a more accurate description. Undoubtedly the best in this group is the all-hair mattress, and also the most costly. Made of the finest black hair, it is filled about a third of the way from one end and then the corners filled out and the hair teased and evened out by hand. This is repeated until the whole mattress is stuffed and then the mouth is sewn up and marked ready for tufting. As with other mattresses, when the tufting is finished two rows of stitching are put around the borders. An all-hair mattress will last many years, is very comfortable and reputedly healthy to sleep upon. To complete the range there are many wool-stuffed mattresses which are comfortable and give excellent service for the average cost.

CHAPTER TWENTY-ONE

Occasional chair—cable sprung

THIS type of chair is very comfortable and is used extensively in the home as a dining-chair, or in the office or showroom. The frame is quite a simple one, a frame that could be tackled by oneself, but the frame-maker will turn them out more quickly and expertly. It requires the minimum amount of stuffing which is very convenient for re-upholstering or only having a change of cover. Note the rebated edges of the side rails and the front rail fixed at a lower level. This lowering of the front rail enables one to include what is virtually a spring edge. This is accomplished by putting three springs close to each other over the edge of the frame, thus giving comfort and softness behind the knees whilst sitting. The cable springs used in this case are material covered and are hooked on to a web-like tape with eyelets punched in. This tape is nailed along the rebated side rails, the fine nails being driven in around the rim of the eyelets. Four or five nails are enough around each eyelet. A block placed under the rail whilst driving in the nails will safeguard against any damage to the woodwork. A lining cover is made for the springs covering the main area of the seat. This is done by hemming the sides and making a slot at each end through which the last and the first cable springs respectively pass. The three edge springs are covered separately and with the cover material proper. A piece of material is cut the width of the seat, plus an inch for side hems, and long enough to go right round the springs and tack under the rail at the front. The hemming is done and the cover is back-tacked on the top ridge of the front rail. It is then taken over the front of the first cable spring and under and over the other two springs to come down to the front and be tacked off under the front rail.

The back is webbed in the orthodox way, interlacing and folding over the webbing. Then a piece of spring

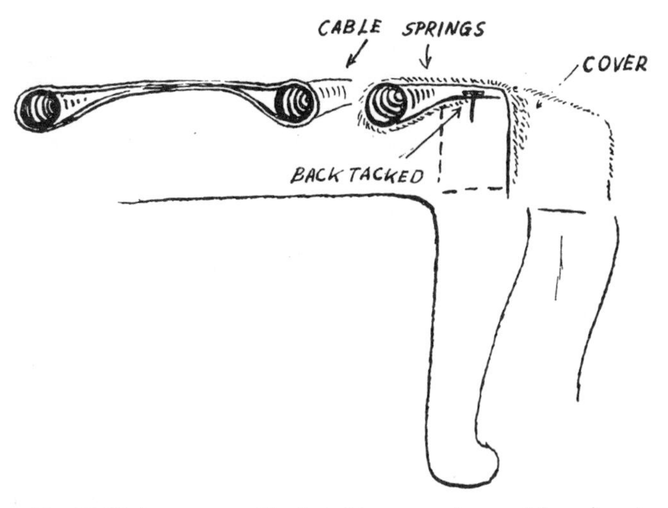

Fig. 25. Lining cover and back-tacking around one cable spring at edge. Same principle is applied to a cluster of three springs.

canvas is tacked over, stretching it as tightly as possible by hand, and again hemming the canvas when tacking off.

The inside edges of the back rail should be rasped to take away the sharp edge. The canvas is covered with a piece of preformed foam rubber and covered with a calico. The cover, which requires no preparation after cutting off, is tacked on the underside of the bottom back rail and strained towards the top rail where it is temporarily tacked, as also are the sides. When satisfied that no further adjustment is needed, the whole of the cover can be tacked off. The outside back is then set in position and either slip-stitched or gimp-pinned right round.

The cushion seat consists of an interior of foam rubber with a calico covering. The two panels and borders are cut to size allowing ½ in. for seaming. The material to form the piping is also cut off and, as for all piping material, it should be cut on the cross. The cushion cover is machined up with a piped edge around both top and bottom panels, leaving one end open to admit the foam-rubber interior. The mouth of the cushion is now slip-stitched to complete the job.

An alternative for the cushion case is to make it a loose cover. This is made up in the same way except that the open end has a strengthening piece of material sewn on the inside border on to which are sewn hooks, whilst the adjoining panel has a piece that carries the eyes or bars for the hooks to fasten up the opening.

CHAPTER TWENTY-TWO

A bedroom chair

HERE is another very simple type of chair that can be used in almost any room in the house. It is mainly seen, however, in the bedroom or bed-sitter and is the right dimensions for use as a nursing-chair. The frame is made of hardwood and the legs are french polished. The front legs can be varied by fixing a 'cabriole' type of leg. Note that the top back rail is slightly curved to take the shape of the shoulders and make a more comfortable back-rest. It is on the back where we commence this time. On the inside of the back rails stretch three or four webs each way, interlacing as usual. Stretch the long webs first, that is from top to bottom, keeping the tacks in the centre of the rails. Now rasp the edges of the back rail on the inside making a facet about ¼ in. Cut off a piece of spring canvas 6 in. longer and wider than the area of the back. Tack this against the facet allowing three inches to hang over on all sides. Tack closely, every ½ in. through the single thickness of the canvas. The extra canvas, overlapping, is for the construction of a thumbroll. With the chair still on its back on the trestles, lay some wool or fibre along the edge evenly, then bring the surplus canvas over and form a roll. The edge of the canvas is turned in and made as firm as possible, pulling it to the edge before tacking it off. This thumbroll wants to be about ¾ in. in diameter, firm and even all round. The corners usually require a little extra time to make a neat job making sure that the roll protrudes over the frame edge just slightly. If it is only the same level the pulling-over of the cover and other materials will cause it to go in and consequently it will lose its proper shape, and the cover will also touch the wood edge.

Sew in two rows at least of twine bridles and fill in with the chosen stuffing. Black wool is quite suitable for a job

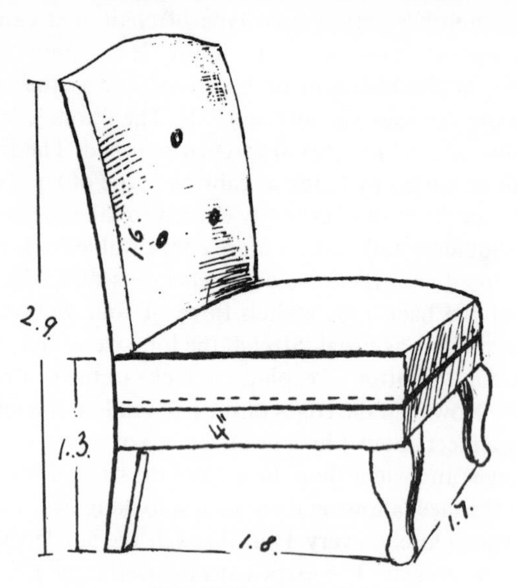

Fig. 26. Bedroom chair.

of this kind but do spend that extra time in 'teasing' it out to get an even surface but with the density of wool slightly more in the centre than elsewhere. This applies to almost every area of stuffing. Tack a piece of hessian over this stuffing, fixing the tacks on to the sides of the rails. Because hessian is that much more open than a canvas it is as well to turn under the edges when tacking. The back is now left and work on the seat begins. A suitable spring unit on metal webs is the seat base. It will consist of about nine springs from 4 to 5 in. in height and have a wire edging around the perimeter. The springs are kept in an upright position by a wire mesh that completely covers the top. This mesh takes the place of lacing. The spring unit is placed in position on top of the seat rails and made secure by driving clout nails through the holes of the wire webbing. A piece of spring canvas is put right over the unit and tacked on the seat rails making a neat corner pleat at the front. This is sewn up at the same time the canvas is looped to the wire edging with twine. Bridle the top of the unit around the edges and a row down the middle. Fill in with fibre stuffing to a depth of about two inches with plenty of overlap at the edges. Cover with a piece of scrim which is held in place by skewers under the wire edge of the unit. Put in the holding ties in the middle of the seat and then commence to build out the edge ready for stitching a roll around. The scrim is turned under when skewering it ready for stitching. A blind stitch is put in which at the same time ties on the scrim under the wire. The stuffing is regulated again and a top stitch inserted to form a roll about 1 in. thick.

The covers for the chair can now be cut off and prepared. If the cover has a pattern, ensure that the motif line continues down the back and along the seat. The inside back will require no flys or piping but is put straight on to the back over a layer of wadding. It is tacked underneath the bottom back rail and stretched up to the top and then the sides are tacked temporarily. When the cover looks right and no further adjustments are required it is tacked off. Upholstery buttons covered with the same material (or a contrast if wanted) can now be put into the back. From two to four buttons can be put in a back of this size, depending on which design appeals—two in the centre, side by side, three in a triangular shape or four making a square or diamond shape. These buttons also act as holding ties for the back stuffing. Mark off where the buttons are going and with a needle and fine twine start from the back by pushing the needle through so that it comes out on the mark on the cover. Take the needle

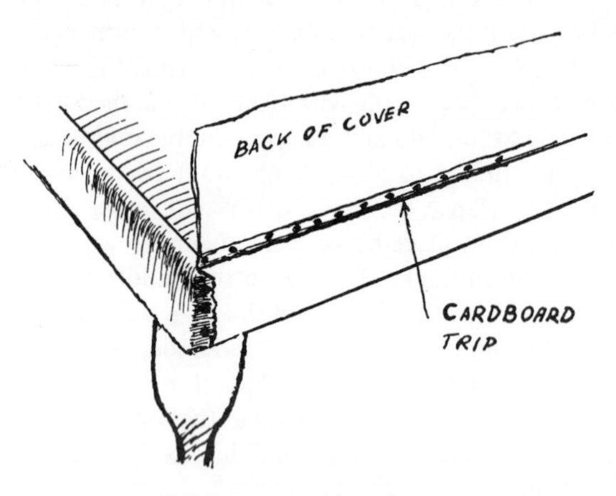

Fig. 27. Back-tacking of cover.

right out and then pass it through the cloth bos on the back of the button. The button is now on the twine and the needle is passed back through the same hole to come out a half-inch away from the point of entry on the back. A slip knot is made and pulled tight and then knotted off securely.

The seat cover has a 5 in. border piped and sewn on, and a fly which goes down on to the back rail. A thin layer of wool or linters felt is put over the first stuffing and the cover pulled over. The fly is tucked down to the back rail and two or three tacks put in to hold it whilst the rest of the cover, particularly the piping, is adjusted. The piping should be resting directly over the edge of the roll. When everything seems to be in place, tack off. The bottom edge of the border is tacked just below the rim of the seat rail. The raw edge of the material is covered by the second border. This second border is approximately 4 in. deep (this allows an inch for tacking) and is piped around the top. The borders of course only go round two sides and the front. This second border is back-tacked around the top edge of the seat rail thus covering the raw edge as mentioned. A guiding line is helpful and this should be parallel to the piped edge of the seat. The second border is tacked off underneath the seat rail. The last piece of cover is now put on, the outside back. This is back-tacked along the top rail, brought over and tacked under the bottom rail. The sides are temporarily tacked until ready for slip-stitching. An alternative is to gimp-pin the sides. A piece of black burlap on the bottom completes the chair.

CHAPTER TWENTY-THREE

Modern tensile-sprung easy-chair

ONE of the most popular types of easy-chair amongst men has always been the long, deep-sprung easy-chair. Sometimes this had side pieces added which are known as 'wings'. A chair that one could relax in, sprawl in and generally find comfort and ease. They can be seen in abundance in almost every club room and indeed came to be known and described as 'club' chairs. These chairs were always a fully upholstered piece of furniture that entailed many hours working time, considerable stuffing amounts and a good yardage of covering material. Made with a 'platform' type of seat and finished off with a feather cushion, they were in great demand. The chairs that did find their way into the clubs were invariably finished in cowhide covering and sometimes in good-quality leathercloth with the feather cushion in the same material or in a good-grade velour of matching colour.

However, the average housewife didn't take to it at all, and at best only looked with favour upon it because of her husband. The reason of course was obvious; it was too big and clumsy and took up far too much room. It certainly was heavy to move around when cleaning the room. The tastes of the housewife and her needs probably influence the furniture manufacturers as much as any other industry and there seems little doubt that the ladies approve very much the modern line that is so much admired in upholstery today. Easy to move because of its lightness in construction, it also presents the minimum of work and expense when covers need replacing, also a reduced yardage in the case of loose covers. All these improvements are achieved without any loss of comfort whatsoever, and the lifetime of the suite or chair is about the same.

Most of these improvements are brought about by smaller frame dimensions, mainly in height, and the adoption of modern hygienic stuffings like rubberized hair, foam rubber and the like. The foundations too have taken advantage of newer and more up-to-date methods of springing. In place of the coil spring there is now either cable springing or tensile webbing and of course the spring unit of all types.

The following chair incorporates one or other of these materials and methods and is an example of the general trend of easy chairs particularly in respect of the qualities of the 'club' chair.

A simple hardwood frame to one's own dimensions, is wanted, and a set of modern legs either in wood or metal can be fixed very easily. These legs usually include some form of ball-bearing castor or metal 'glide plate' for easy movement. These modern castors also protect the carpeting.

The seat and back will be sprung with tensile webbing. The back webbing is put on first and tacked, or rather nailed with fine but fairly large-headed nails, directly on to the frame, on the inside. With this rubber webbing a hem of course is not necessary but it is better to nail through some kind of tough material before the web. In this case, as it will not be seen, strips of ordinary webbing about 1 in. wide could be placed over the rubber webbing where the nails have to pierce. Some four or five webs each way, interlaced, will do the back. The sides or inside arms are next webbed, but with orthodox webbing. Four pieces of webbing are stretched vertically on the inside of the rails, placing the last web about 2 in. from the back rail. This will form the opening or 'gap' through

Fig. 28. Modern tensile-sprung chair.

which the cover and flys will go. Cover now with a piece of spring canvas, tacking on the inside rails and again leaving the opening at the last web free. Two straight cuts here and the surplus canvas is taken through the gap and tucked behind the web temporarily. The edges of the long arm should now be rasped both inside and outside. On the inside arm a shallow layer of rubberized hair or foam rubber is tacked just reaching to the level of the arm-rest. On top of the arm-rest an inch-thick layer of rubber is laid extending from the back to the bottom of the facing. This can be kept in position by bands of adhesive tape or again tacking to the framework. Cover the inside arm and arm-rest with calico, tacking to the inside bottom rail and on the outside of the arm-rest rail. Both arms should be brought to this stage before returning to the back. The back is designed to have a preformed foam-rubber stuffing. This will be shaped as the back frame but with the front area slightly bigger overall, which will mean the outside line is slightly proud of the back rail dimensions. The thickness of this preformed rubber back can be from 2 to 3 in. and is enclosed in a calico casing to which a tape has been sewn into the seams. This tape, which is on the smaller panel of the casing, is used to attach the foam rubber to the frame by tacking it on to the outside of the back rails all round.

The seat edge is a little wider than on the majority of chairs as far as the frame goes, and this is also covered with a layer of foam rubber with a piece of calico put over, thus forming a 'platform' edge to match the subsequent foam cushion.

The cutting and preparing of the cover material is now done. The inside back is cut to the shape of the front panel of foam rubber, and piped on to it is a border extending from one arm-rest, around the top, to the next arm-rest. The piping of this back panel, however, starts from the corner of the seat, curves around the shape of the arm-rest, around the top border to continue and end at the opposite corner of the seat. Where the piping commences to curve around the arms a 'fly' consisting of half material, half canvas is sewn. This pulls out of sight into the tuck-away adjoining arm and back, and goes through the 'gap' to be tacked against the face of the main back rail. The inside arms, the long arm-rests and facings, and the outside arms are made in one, jacket style. The inside arm panel is cut to go from the top arm rail to the tacking rail only, where it is turned and tacked either on the inside face of the rail or out of sight underneath. The cushion panels are cut along with the borders and also a piece for the front border, which should match in line with the cushion, which in turn has been matched with the back panel. To keep a desired softness to the arm line, it will be better to make up the arm jackets without piping them but just stitching the seams twice for added strength. Before machining these pieces it is necessary to position them on the arm and to notch them here and there so that they can be matched in place on the machine.

The piece of cover for the front edge and border is now put on. This can be back-tacked along the edge of the front rail, covering the nailed ends of the rubber webbings of the seat. Bring over the cover and tack under the front rail. The sides on top of the edge are turned under but those on the face are allowed to extend on to the facing and are tacked. The prepared inside back can now be put on over a layer of wadding. This is set in position with one or two tacks holding it until the right position is attained. The first consideration is to see that the piped edging lies over the line of the foam-rubber unit. When this is accomplished, tack the base of the cover to the bottom rail, either underneath or on the face of the tacking rail. Next take the flys through the gap and tack off against the face of the main back rail, making sure there are no rucks, and if necessary stuffing out with wadding any hollow spots around the curved piping. The top border will require building up with a layer or two of wadding before pulling taut and tacking off. Now the outside arm can have a piece of canvas tacked over the area between the top rail and the tacking rail. This will act as a strengthening lining for the outside arm cover. Cover with wadding the whole area and pull on the jacketed cover. Set in position with the seams along the arm line and stretch from the back of the arm to the base of the facing or top arm. When satisfied with the fitting, turn in the edge of the inside panel and tack along the face of the tacking rail. This rail is almost on the same level as the front rail so the finished edge of this panel will rest and meet the turned-in side edge of the front border. At this point also you will have to turn in the raw edge of the top arm and temporary-tack it for the last few inches to the bottom rail. Later it is slip-stitched. Next go to the back, make two straight cuts, take the cover through the gap and tack off on top of the back fly. Finish the adjusting of the rest of the cover by tacking off under the side rail and on the outside of the back rail. The outside back cover is temporarily tacked on and later slip-stitched, whilst the cushion has its cover pulled on and the mouth sewn up. Remember to plug out the corners of the cushion if necessary with cotton wool to maintain the sharp clean lines of the chair. The bottom will need no black hessian, for the rubber webbings like the back webs are tacked on top of their respective rails.

It is much neater to turn in the edges of the material that has been taken under the base rail to be tacked.

This is a chair well within the range even of the amateur and one that will give pleasure and a great amount of comfortable relaxation.

There are many places where foam rubber can be bought at reasonable prices, especially off-cuts, end of-range shapes, etc. If the cost of ordering specially shaped pieces seems too much one can, with a little patience (and the upholsterer has a lot of this), a 3 in. roll of adhesive tape and liquid latex rubber, make up almost any shape required.

12. *Above:* This traditional English design by Parker-Knoll is well loved. The two-seater settee and wing easy-chair are upholstered in the modern manner and lose nothing of the comfort that this design conveys. The legs are finished in Antique walnut or Mahogany.

CHAPTER TWENTY-FOUR

Adaptable settee unit

A NEW type of seating arrangement has developed in the home since the advent of television. Very soon after television had established itself on the home market, it was seen that a smaller type of chair was needed so that people could have a suitable view whilst watching their entertainment. The chairs were put side by side as closely as possible and it was much more intimate for the family. This smaller style of chair soon became very popular not only in the home, but in pubs, hotels and clubs, in fact anywhere that people congregated for the purpose of watching television. Once it had established itself this chair was adapted to many other uses, and it wasn't long before the designers created the 'settee units'. These were simply three or four chairs that could be put side by side to give the appearance of a settee. Sometimes they are seen forming a curve or in a three- or four-sided settee with about a 60 degree bend. It certainly makes a very useful addition to any home, being able to ring the changes not only in the number of units but also by having alternative coverings for perhaps half the units.

The unit described is a simple design but it will be seen that other variations can be used, in the structure of the front legs for example, or perhaps a shaped back depending upon one's taste in design or comfort. It is made from hardwood and has a slightly stuffed back, cable springing for the seat, surmounted with a foam-rubber cushion interior. The covers can be cut immediately for this chair or chairs and will consist of the outside back and inside back pieces; two pieces for the high side rails and a small border to cover the cluster of three cable springs over the front of the chair; two cushion panels and

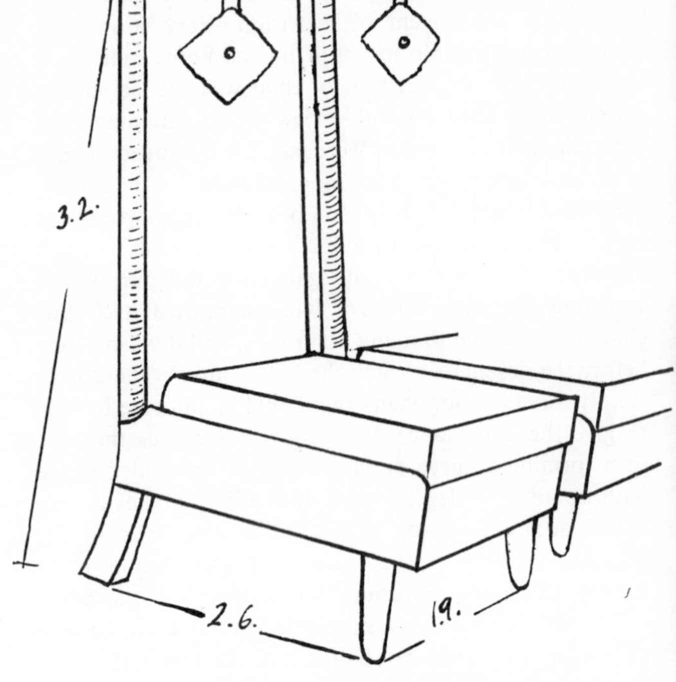

Fig. 29. The adaptable settee unit.

borders, and then two pieces for the neck cushion with a piece of waste to make the strapping to hold it. This completes the material needed, but a platform of lining is wanted to cover the cable springing of the main part of the seat. The only machining to be done is the small side hems on the front border, the hemming and pockets of the lining, and of course the making-up and piping of the cushions and the piece of strapping. The side rails are rebated on the inside to carry the web-type eyelets which are nailed with fine nails on to this rebated ledge, the nails going around the rim of the eyelets. Two matching tapes are therefore fixed for about five cable springs. The front rail has the same base line as the sides but is only half the height and the edge is formed by fixing closely together three cable springs. Two of these springs are on top of the edge and one on the border as it were.

The side rail cover is put on first, turning in the edge and tacking along the rebated wood close to the eyelet tape. It is then brought over the sides and tacked underneath the rail and around the back rail. When both sides are tacked it might be as well to do the front border piece. This piece of cover is back-tacked on the inside of the low front rail, using a strip of cardboard on the back of the cover before tacking. It is then brought in front of the first cable spring and under the other two springs to fold over them and return down the front and be tacked under the front rail. The same method is shown in the sketch but using only one cable spring and with a front rail that is the same height as the side rails.

The inside edges of the back rails should be rasped to take away any sharpness. It is then webbed with ordinary webbing on the inside—four webs down the length and five webs across, not forgetting to interlace them. A length of spring canvas covers the webbing and is tacked in the way described, with an overlap. A fairly substantial layer of rubberized hair is then kept on by four or five holding ties in the centre. It is now covered with calico or hessian. Over this is put a layer of linters felt and the cover can now be fixed. Tack first on the inside of the bottom tacking rail, turning in the edge of the material, then stretch towards the top rail and temporarily tack all round. When satisfied the cover is placed properly, tack off. The material is also turned as it meets the side rail pieces and is either gimp-pinned or slip-stitched. A neat pleat is put in at the top corners making sure it doesn't show a bump. The outside back can now be back-tacked in position ready to be slip-stitched and the first and last cable springs put in the slots of the lining cover. The foam rubber cushion is put in its case and the mouth sewn up. No black burlap is required underneath and therefore all material that is tacked under the rails should be turned in and finished neatly.

The neck cushion is approximately 9 in. square. It will have a piped edge and two upholstery buttons to keep the kapok in place. A doubled piece of material sewn together forms a strapping and is sewn in with the piping at one corner. At the end of the strap a press stud is attached which connects with its other half which is nailed on to the top rail.

CHAPTER TWENTY-FIVE

Upholstery repairs

THE basic operations for repairing any part of a suite, or any of the pieces that have already been written about, of course remain the same, depending on what has to be done. There is always some ripping-out to be done and if it is a complete re-upholstering job then the whole of the frame is laid bare. If it is only for the covers to be replaced then only the covers, including the outside covers, will have to come off.

The majority of repair jobs only need new seats putting in, and again many seats that only require new webbing and perhaps a spring or two. The need for re-webbing is usually the result of heavy punishment or faulty webbing technique, including the use of inferior-grade webbing. However, it is policy to examine the frame carefully and make sure that there is no other reason for the failure of the seat foundation, such as sharp edges of the frame or rough wire knots on the springs. A close examination of the old webbing will show either of these faults.

Salvaging as much material as possible is a common practice in workshops but it is carefully done and materials are not used again merely for the sake of saving money. Each piece of canvas or hessian and each spring is only re-used if it is considered that the soundness of such components is unimpaired.

Before the details are discussed there is the importance of ripping-out to be stressed—that is, the importance of ripping-out correctly. This is done with a 'ripping chisel' and a wooden mallet. The chisel being held at an angle, with the blade edge pointing under the edge of the tack head. The top of the chisel handle is then struck one or two sharp blows by the mallet, which will remove the tack. This becomes a continuous and easy operation after very short practice. Always rip out along the grain of the wood and not across it. This will mean that when you reach the junction of rails you must change your position and

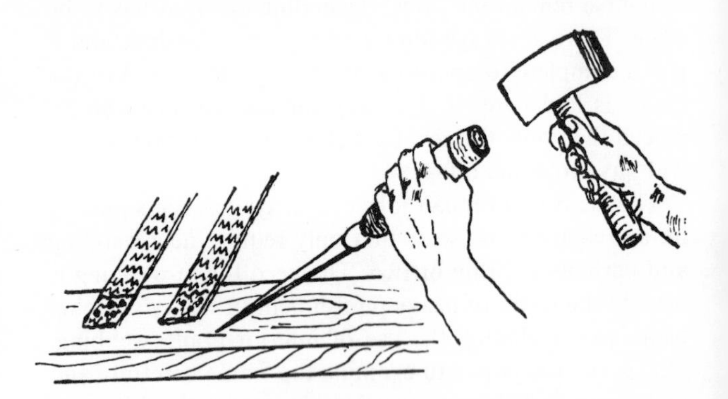

Fig. 30. Using the ripping-out tools.

knock out the few remaining tacks in the opposite direction from which you have been working. If attempts are made to knock out corner tacks outwards then certainly pieces of the frame will be chipped off. This can cause extra work in repairs, particularly with small chairs such as dining-chairs where it is necessary to have an even-stitched edge.

The carding of stuffings if they are to be re-used can be a very dusty task unless some type of carding machine is available. The decision as to the re-use of stuffings is of course governed by its condition and age. If there is a lot of dust caused purely by the disintegration of the stuffing through age, then the best policy is to scrap it and use new fibres or hairs. If, however, the stuffing materials are still strong and springy they are probably quite good for many more years and after being carded can be used with confidence. The larger workshop will most likely have a power machine which serves the bedding section mainly as well as the upholstery workshop. It usually has a slatted wooden conveyor belt that carries the caked stuffing underneath a pair of heavy rollers embedded with spikes at regular intervals. These rollers card the stuffing and at the same time the dust is extracted through an air vent. Sometimes, if the stuffing is very hard, it may require a double journey through the machine. It is returned underneath the conveyor belt into a bin. A smaller type of machine and manually operated is also used. It is on the same principle but the roller is turned by a handle similar to that used on an old-fashioned wringing machine. If neither of these machines is available old stuffing is broken up into pieces and then beaten with a stick. This needs to be carried out in an airy place so that the dust can freely disperse. It is finished off when actually being put under the bridles, by hand teasing; in other words, pulling out any further 'tats' and evening out the stuffing.

Dining-chair

In all repair jobs that are to have the same cover replaced, care must be taken when removing the cover. This applies particularly to the small chair such as a dining-chair as the whole of the cover is seen and therefore it is not possible to add pieces if it is tight. In the case of easy-chairs, etc., where flys are sewn on, very often a new canvas fly is machined on for strength and to give that extra inch for pulling the cover into position. With the dining-chair the cover is net all around and particularly where the back rails and the seat rails meet. The cover has been cut at this point in order to fall round the rail, and the apex of this cut is likely to be a weak point. The trestles usually have the board bench over them for small chairs. Turn over the chair and commence to rip off the black hessian cover on the bottom, and the webbings. The webbings, incidentally, are never any use for replacing on the same area as there is not enough length to stretch them properly. But if they are in good condition they can be kept for other jobs such as spring edges, tacking over supporting rails, etc. When the canvas bottom is off and the webs freed from tacks, cut off the webs from the springs and then cut out the springs from the canvas. Retain any good springs and dispose of the remainder. An old spring is sometimes straightened out to obtain a long piece of wire to act as a substitute for a cane edge, but it is not a very satisfactory substitute. In testing old springs for further service, place them upright on the bench and put the palm of the hand over the top coil. Press down quickly and firmly and if they break away quickly from a straight downwards movement they should be discarded. However, if they go down fairly straight and return with a good spring they will probably be good enough to use again. Still with the chair upside down on the bench continue to rip out the tacks holding the cover and gimp. This is where extra care should be taken in order not to damage any show-wood there may be. As soon as the cover and any calico is removed, stand the chair up on the bench to complete the ripping-out. This will be the first-stuffing hessian and the spring canvas covering. The twine bridles are snipped in order to remove the second stuffings and also the holding ties and bridles to remove the first stuffing from the spring canvas. The spring canvas is examined to see if it can be used again and also the first and second stuffings. If it is decided to use the stuffing then the scrim is removed. This can be done by just pulling away the fibre or first cutting all the stitches before removing it. You may decide to do the latter if it is a very good scrim which might be used again, if not for the chair then for some smaller job.

To strip the chair in this manner and deal with each piece of material is a tidier way than ripping out everything first and then separating them after the innards are away from the frame. However, it may save time if, for instance, the cabinet maker is waiting to do some repair to the frame before it can be re-stuffed. This brings us now to the frame which should be examined to see if everything is sound. Joints and dowels should be tested and, if found to be loose, they should be opened a little, glued and cramped afresh. It may also be that the legs and show-wood of the frame require polishing before one can again start on them. Whilst these jobs are going on it is just as well to have the stuffing carded ready for use when required.

When the frame is ready, lay upside down on the bench and commence webbing in the usual way, three or four webs interlaced and the ends folded over. The springs are then placed and sewn in. If any old springs are being used they should be put in whatever corner they had a tendency to lean towards. Even if all the springs are good it is the practice to put in one new spring in the centre of the seat. Lace them together and tack over the spring canvas, not pulling it too tightly. Next sew the canvas to the top coils of the springs. Bridle and fill in the stuffing, using any extra new that may be needed. The holding ties are put in and the edge formed and stitched. This is a point in the renovation that should be checked for dimensions, for remember that the old cover may be going back. The newly stuffed seat doesn't want to be an inch wider for example—or for that matter an inch longer. This same consideration is given when filling in the second stuffing. When re-upholstering and using the same cover it is always a help to cover with calico, for the greater strain of the bulk of stuffing is contained within the calico covering. This makes it easier to adjust the cover and consequently less strain is put upon it. A new piece of black burlap is put on the bottom, and new gimp or banding pinned around the edging. If the stuffing and the stitched edge are in good order then of course the whole of the stuffing can be replaced *en bloc* on top of the springs or on top of the canvas if it is not sprung. Holding ties are put in and the tacked burlap is strengthened by making a stitch right round and looping the twine round a tack and driving home. This of course saves a lot of time in stitching and stuffing. There are also times when the stitched stuffing is in excellent condition but the hessian is not. In this case the entire stuffing is covered with a fresh piece of hessian and tacked closely right round. An additional top stitch is usually put in to prevent the burlap moving too much.

Now and again one may be required to re-upholster one of these occasional chairs that are close studded right around. The ripping chisel should be used very carefully with this type of furniture, and it is best to lift out these studs or nails rather than knock them out, as damage to the show-wood will invariably happen. It is a long and tedious task lifting out these round-headed nails but it can have an advantage inasmuch as perhaps three-quarters of the nails can be salvaged and used again.

Loose seats have to be set against a fixed edge or block to prevent them moving when being ripped out. When once the cover is off, however, the canvas and webbings can be knocked off by standing the seat on edge and using the claw end of the hammer to knock out the tacks. After new webs and canvas, the stuffing of a loose seat can always be used, using some new to bolster it out. Where new covers are to be used the cutting of them can be taken from the old covers. However, allow at least an inch extra all round, for remember the old cover has been stretched and you do want at least a fingerhold to tack on the new.

Easy-chairs

If the chair or chairs are to have new covers then all the tacks holding the old covers should be ripped out but the cover left on until each part of the chair is ready to receive the new cover. The outside back and the outside arms, however, can be taken off, and of course if it is a complete job of re-stuffing then the complete frame should be stripped of all stuffing and material and examined for any repairs, as in the case of the small dining type of chair. Most chairs come into the workshop for a new seat only, the old cover going back on. The procedure is to turn over the chair and commence ripping off the black hessian bottom, the webbings and any tacks holding the covers. The outside covers are released as far up as the tacking rails, lifted up and kept in position with a couple of tacks. You now have access to releasing the flys in order to take out the seat. In the case of an easy-chair with a spring edge many upholsterers prefer to knock out the whole seat before stripping off the webs, springs, etc. This is because the spring edge can't be removed anyway, before the canvas and burlap are removed.

Separate the stuffings and hessians and salvage any springs to be used again. It is never worth while retaining an old stitched roll for it entails just as much time in re-stitching it beneath the cane edge as it would forming a new one. Examine the main joints of the frame to see if they have any play in them. If so knock them apart slightly, glue and cramp them. The old fibre and hair, or whatever stuffing was used, should be carded in readiness and any extra springs needed are selected to match up with the old ones. New flys are nearly always wanted and in any case it makes it easier to work with new flys sewn on.

Once the chair is ready and the preparations completed, turn the chair upside down and start to web the seat, interlacing four or five webs each way in the same manner as described earlier. Set out the springs with the new ones in the centre of the seat. Some of the old springs may be leaning a certain way; try to place them towards the corners but not with the wire knots on the outside. Lace them with a laid cord and proceed to form the spring edge, remembering to tack a piece of webbing along the front rail to stop any sound of the coils striking the wood. A new piece of spring canvas is always needed for a platform seat and this is duly tacked on, making the necessary guttering and then sewing the canvas to the top coils of the springs and the cane edge looped with twine. The bridles are inserted to take the stuffing and covered with scrim. Holding ties and the stitched roll along the front will complete the scrim stuffing. The second stuffing is put on and the cover with the new flys sewn on is pulled over. The older type of easy-chair may well have a single (or double) border put on separately from the main platform seat; i.e. a lining seat with approximately 5 in. cover along the edge. The cover is attached to the seat by sewing along the seam of the 'lining and cover' and the main part of the seat tacked off in the normal way. The

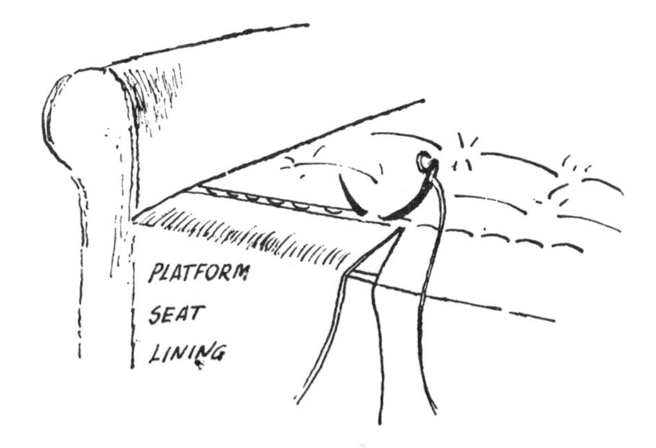

Fig. 31. Sewing on platform seat cover.

small piece of cover going over the roll, however, is slightly different. It is brought over the edge and skewered to hold, and the ends are brought down the outside of the end springs of the spring edge. A neat small pleat is put at the corners and the extension pieces down the sides are stuffed out until they are against the sides of the facings. The edge is sewn on to the border spring canvas with twine. Bridles are then put in the border ready for the stuffing. The front edge of the cover (which was skewered, remember) is now slip-stitched with twine along the underside of the roll. After the border is stuffed, a layer of wadding is put over and the single or double border is skewered at the top and tacked under the base rail. The border is then slip-stitched under the roll and the sides, with fine twine or linen thread and finished off with a furniture cord, this too being sewn on. Any remaining flys of the arms or back which may have been removed from their tacks are now retacked into position again and the outside covers dropped and refixed. A new piece of black hessian is tacked on to complete the installation of a new seat. It may be that a spring-unit interior cushion may need attention or perhaps a feather cushion requires additional feathers to set up the easy-chair for many more years of service.

Very often an easy-chair might only require one or two new seat springs and a re-web. Only the burlap base and the webs need to be ripped out. When this is done cut the lacing cords very carefully where they cross over each other on the centre springs. Undo the knots on as many of the springs that have to be replaced and then cut the springs from the canvas. When cutting through the ties holding them be careful not to cut the canvas. Replace with new springs of the same height and gauge. These are put in one at a time and are sewn in with a half-circular needle over the old mark made by the original spring. This is rather a fiddly and tedious task but if it is worth while it must be done thoroughly. After the springs are attached firmly another awkward job is to lace the old laid cord back on as far as it will go. An extra piece of cord will have to be knotted on. The two ends will meet approximately near the point of where they were cut. Next start webbing the seat again. Do not worry about pushing the springs under the webs and in place until all the webbing is completed. The springs are then worked under the webs and pushed into position to be sewn into the webs by the half-circular needle and fine twine. Fine twine is usually used double as the eye of the half-circular needle is not as big as that of the spring needle and won't easily take the medium twine. It also makes the sewing of the springs easier when using this type of needle. The sewing of the springs follows the same pattern as normally followed; that is, three ties to each coil and knotted separately. A new black burlap bottom completes the renovation. This repair is usually brought about by the use of inferior-grade webbing and this is apparent when ripping out. Nothing but the best-quality webbing is worth putting on when repairing.

Deep-buttoned Chesterfield or Davenport

I am including these in the re-upholstery section as they are pieces that last many years and for some are the last word in comfort and style. And indeed when a good specimen is covered with a good material it presents an elegant example of traditional English furniture. Before entering on the working details it might be as well to remind the reader of the two types of buttoning. 'Float' buttoning is when the upholstery buttons just make a slight indentation to the cover whilst deep buttoning can vary from 1 in. to 2 in. deep into the stuffed back or seat. It is with this latter style that the detail of re-upholstering such a Chesterfield deals.

The Chesterfield settee, or Davenport as it is usually called in America, has a fairly deep, well-sprung seat with a spring edge. The back and arms are in one, and form a continuous line around the Chesterfield at a constant height. Sometimes they are stuffed level in the normal way but many are deep-buttoned. The re-upholstering of the seat or back, which is also sprung, is very little different from any other type of re-upholstery. It is certainly much larger and of course entails many man-hours as far as labour goes. The basic principles are the same but extra care and patience are required on the longer spring edge and also on the back springing particularly. The springing of the back is carried out with a light-gauge spring which comes up from the seat level right over to the outside edge of the frame, making the top of the back and arms as wide as 9 to 12 in. These back springs are laced loosely in order to retain softness. A shallow but firm scrim stuffing is in hair and the second, and more voluminous stuffing is always in the best-quality hair. The time-taking work of this type of settee is naturally the deep-buttoning on of the cover. This also varies according to the kind of cover chosen. There are Chesterfields covered in cowhide and this certainly takes many hours and lasts for years, but hardly seems the right choice for such furniture. Another difficult cover is velour which must be placed just right to get the folds even and not twisted.

We will mainly deal with the attaching of the cover. The back and arms are done first in three separate pieces of cover, the centre part and two arm parts. If the job is only a re-cover with new material, the buttoning depressions in the second stuffing will already be there to guide you, but if it has been restuffed then of course the buttoning plan or design should be marked out on the scrim stuffing. After the second stuffing and wadding is on, the plan is followed by hollowing the hair and making a hole in the wadding over the button points. This gives a guidance when sewing in the buttons. A similar guide must be marked on the cover if a satisfactory result is to be achieved. It soon becomes obvious that a length of cover from A to B must have a liberal allowance if it is to be deep-buttoned. How much that allowance has to be can depend upon the depth of the buttons but is usually anything from a third to a half extra fullness. So, for example, if the nett measurement from the two extreme points on the back is 6 ft., then the required length would need to be from 8 to 9 ft. long and of course a proportionate allowance for the size, from over the top of the back, to the point where it meets the seat and the flys are sewn on. On the back of each piece of cover the plan for buttoning is marked, but although the design may correspond with the one on the scrim stuffing it will be larger because it is done a third to a half bigger. When the second stuffing has been put on and the wadding covered (with the holes put in), the centre part of the cover is laid on in position and the buttoning started from the centre to work away from in both directions. It is usually a diamond pattern and the folds of the material are turned inwards or facing towards the shallower part of the design. This art of buttoning requires infinite patience, the ability to visualize the completed design and plenty of good 'regulating' of the hair stuffing to the right places. When the mitres at the junction of back and arms are reached the cover is allowed to overlap on to the arms a little and the join is made naturally by the diamond pattern when the arm pieces are put on. Pleats are formed from each button along the bottom row as the cover is taken under the tacking rail and tacked off. The same thing also applies to the top row of buttons. Starting from the centre keep the pleats facing opposite ways as they continue around the back and arms to the facings. If the seat is also deep-buttoned then the same procedure is adopted with the buttoning; in this instance the pleats go from each button on the outside rows down to the back base rail for tacking, and over the front edge for sewing under the roll. A complete buttoned Chesterfield also includes the border, but this is a single row of buttons placed centrally along the length with vertical pleats. Not many of these fully buttoned Chesterfields are found but quite a number with the buttoned back and plain balloon-type seat are about still, and also the plain Chesterfield with plain seat and back. In this example the three parts of the back cover are mitred at 45 degrees and the mitre sewn with a piping if fancied, as also are the outside edges of the facings. To mitre the cover, lay the material in position on the back. This piece of cover will probably consist of a width of 48 in. material with a fill-out on either side of a quarter or half width. Remember the length has to stretch from the extreme corner rails around at the back of the Chesterfield. It should be mentioned that this preparation is done either at the scrim stuffing stage or over a calico covering. A line is marked or a piece of twine fixed to show the line of the mitre and when the covers are skewered or temporary-tacked in position they are cut to this line with an allowance of ½ in. for seaming together. The outside cover is also done in this way making the mitre down the centre of the corner rails and in line with the inside cover mitre.

Folding screens

Although this is not strictly a piece of upholstered furniture it is a job that is done by the upholsterer, and it is not uncommon to get them into the workshop for recovering. There are many varieties of screen from the elaborate show-wood frames with mirror top panels to the ordinary three- or four-panel screen covered in coloured jute material. The commonest kind are of four sections joined by hinges folding one way only. These are about 5 ft. 9 in. high and each section about 15 in. wide and made up of timber 2 in. × $\frac{3}{4}$ in. The first thing to do when having to re-cover is to separate the sections by unscrewing the hinges. The cover is then ripped off, not torn off, of course, but every tack and gimp pin removed by use of the ripping chisel and mallet. Depending on the quality of the old cover you may have quite a number of gimp pins to remove. A pair of pincers will also be wanted to remove some of these. Extra care is always required when ripping out these screens for the edges can be easily damaged and this will mean more repairs. There is no stuffing and as the cover goes directly against the frame any discrepancy does show up. Once all the tacks are cleared, inspect the frame for loose joints and any pieces that may have come off. Repair and glue where needed before proceeding. Sandpaper down any rough or sharp edges that may have been caused when ripping out. Each section has now what might be described as three square windows. Cover these windows on both sides of the frame with brown paper. Cut out the pieces for each window or opening, making them about two inches bigger all round. Next, glue around the opening about two inches in, using hot glue and stick on the brown paper. Immediately it is on, damp the centre of the paper. As this dries it will give a taut and sound covering for these openings. Treat each section in the same way. The extent of the next stage of work largely depends on the quality of the covering to go on. But even for the lesser grade of cover the frame is covered with a hessian on both sides. This is stretched hand-tight and each side tacked separately on the outside edge of the frame with three-eighths tacks. Do not cover the recessed part where the hinges are screwed. In place of hessian, interlining, commonly known as Bump in the curtain section of upholstery, can be used. The panels of cover material are now cut off and if patterned they must be carefully matched so that each section shows the main motif evenly. The cover can be put on in the same way as the hessian or interlining, i.e. tacked on to the outside edge of the frame and then a banding or wide gimp put round to cover the tacked edge. An alternative method is to put on one panel of the cover by tacking on the edge and the facing panel to come right over the edge and be either gimp-pinned round or temporary-tacked until slip-stitched right round with thread. The latter way certainly makes for the better-class finish. In both methods the hinge plates are covered with either the material or banding, so it is better to leave finishing the hinged sides until the screen has been assembled again. With the better-quality screen or cover even the hinge joint is covered. This is usually done with a strip of the cover or a strip of lining. Fold the screen closed and along the two edges where the hinge joint shows sew the strip of covering. One or two gimp pins down the inside edges will ensure that this strip will fold inwards when the screen is opened out. As mentioned at the start of this chapter, a very elaborate screen can call for a lot of hand-sewing by the upholstress. Except in the smaller workshop the upholstress now deals only with curtain work and in some cases loose cover work. Her work in the stuffing shop has been curtailed greatly with the changing styles of furniture and the advent of 'jacketed' covers. This has done away with, for example, all cording work. After a suite had been finished or repaired it was put on trestles ready for the upholstress to sew furniture cord around the facings, along the borders, etc., as a finish. The popularity of the cleaner machined piped edge did away with all this hand work. Of course the amount of machining is greater but it is not unusual to find a youth doing this job nowadays whilst the greater skill and patience usually found in any seamstress is utilized on drapery work and loose covers.

It is always surprising when one comes across a piece of furniture not known of or not seen before. It is not long ago that I saw for the first time a type of foot-rest and leg-rest combined. It was T shaped, the top part of the T about 18 in. long by 9 in. wide and about 1 in. thick. The two ends were slightly curved inwards. Rising from the centre the stalk of the T was of similar dimensions but each side was padded. The whole stool was covered in a material and had a leather carrying handle tacked on to the end of the padded part. What was it for? The answer, a 'gout stool'. As the afflicted person sat in the easy chair the heel of the foot rested in the curved part whilst the calf of the leg rested upon the padded section, the great advantage being that by moving the leg slightly a new restful angle could be found for the leg or gouty foot.

Although style and design have changed much in the last ten years and manufacturers have adopted readily the new materials for the manufacture of upholstered furniture, there is now a tendency for the older design to become popular again. In many stores one sees a smaller deep-buttoned suite, but with a curved line both in the back and the seat. Another good seller is the heavily rouched suite with a rouched piping around 'down' cushions on both seats and backs. One thing is quite clear, the public are catered for on all levels and are given a better-quality job and better value for money than ever before.

13. *Above:* This award-winning design of the 'Heritage' by Uniflex is an excellent example of modern design and upholstery. The length is broken by the four cushions and the graduated slope of the back and arms. This plate shows how well completely different designs, as of the two easy-chairs, can blend with each other. When sitting in these chairs there is no pressure on the calves.

CHAPTER TWENTY-SIX

Terminology

As in any other craft or trade there are a number of words or phrases that are either outside normal language or perhaps known words that convey a completely different meaning. Many technical words and terms never find their way into the ordinary dictionary and unless ready reference is available it sometimes means that interest can be lost or a wrong interpretation put on a word that means lost time in study. In this chapter I have drawn up a list of such words.

Perhaps a recapitulation of the names and abbreviations of the cover pieces of an average chair or suite would be as well to start off such a chapter. These names I shall keep together in a group regardless of alphabetical order. Most are self-explanatory.

Item	*Abbreviation and/or description*
SEAT	St.
INSIDE BACK	I.B.
OUTSIDE BACK	O.B.
INSIDE ARM	I.A.
OUTSIDE ARM	O.A.
BORDER	Bdr. Can be in front or along top of back.
FACINGS	Fcgs. The front of the arm-rests. Can also be on the sides of a back.
PLATFORM SEAT	Pl. St. A Platform Seat is one that has a guttering and has a cushion.

BLACK AND WHITE WEBBING	Best English webbing with herring-bone design.
BOS	A projection from the back of an upholstery button. Made of cloth to enable a needle and twine to pass through.
BRIDLING	A series of twine loops about six inches long which are put in canvases to carry the stuffing and keep it in position.
BUFFED	The rubbing or buffing with carborundum to obviate any blemishes that may be in hides.
BUTTONING	The insertion of upholstery buttons. Two methods used are 'Float' Buttoning and 'Deep' Buttoning. The former method leaves the button on the face of the cover, whilst the latter is pulled into the cover deeply and forms a pleated diamond.
CABRIOLE	Name given to a hammer with a small driving area. Used mainly on show-wood furniture.
FLYS	Pieces of hessian or any old material sewn on to the inside edges of the cover material to save material and give added strength for pulling cover into position. Known as 'Pull-throughs' in U.S.A.
GAP	Name used in describing the opening between the arm web

and the back upright rail. Left free for passing through flys, etc., to be tacked against rail.

GAUGE — Applied to the thickness of the steel wire in the manufacture of coil springs. See chapter 4.

HOLDING TIE — A stitch between the spring canvas and scrim. Keeps the first stuffing firmly in place. Also known as 'Through Stitch'.

JACKETS — One or more parts joined together to form a tailored finish, e.g. inside arm and facing.

LACING — A term applied to the stringing together of coil springs in which a 'laid' cord is used.

LININGS — Pieces of old canvas tacked on to the outsides before the outside covers are put on. Gives extra resistance to pressure, especially needed in the case of leather covering. Not to be confused with the outside covers proper, which are known as 'linings' in America.

PIPING FOOT — An attachment for the sewing machine to enable piped edges to be sewn on to joins.

PULLTHROUGH — Meaning the same as a FLY. An American Term.

RAILS
STRETCHER — A supporting rail on a settee or divan base.

TACKING — The lighter rails for tacking foundations and covers to.

BASE — The main foundation rail at floor level.

REBATED — Where a groove is put in the edge of a rail, and the lower edge used for tacking, or where cable springing is fixed.

REGULATING — The 'working about' of stuffing to the required place for stitching, etc.

RIPPING OUT — Procedure for stripping chairs for repair.

SCRIM STUFFING — Another term for the first stuffing enclosed in scrim or hessian.

SHOW-WOOD — Polished wood surrounding to stuffed or upholstered part of furniture, as with a dining-chair or occasional chair.

SKIVING — The art of chamfering a piece of hide in order to join together two pieces by gluing.

SPRING EDGE — Mostly applies to the front edge of chairs, but also to all edges where an independent springing is adopted.

SPRING INTERIOR — The inside springing of a cushion or mattress.

SPRING UNIT — A collection of springs to form foundations for seats, arms and backs. Wired and clipped together. See chapter 4.

STITCHING — The stitching by twine of edges and

rolls to form a shape to stuffing. See chapter 11.

STRAPS — Metal bands or webs upon which spring units are mounted and fixed to the frame by clout nails.

TACK DRAWS — The 'shadowed' furrow caused by the strain of a tack. Particularly on silk covers.

TEMPORARY TACKS — Tacks only half driven in. Easily removed.

TENSILE — Applies to rubber webbing or cable-springing.

THUMBROLL — An alternative to a stitched edge. Known as a cordroll by the American upholsterer.

TUFTING — Carried out on mattresses. Same procedure as in buttoning.

WIRE KNOTS — The finish of the metal coil on a spring.

These represent the majority of terms used in the upholstery trade. Once again I must point out that this book is dealing purely with the part of the trade known as the 'Stuffers'. The soft furnishing and carpet departments also have their own particular terminology.

Index